AF866000

Deep Learning with Emerging Engineering Applications

Edited by Ali Akdagli

Published in London, United Kingdom

Deep Learning with Emerging Engineering Applications
http://dx.doi.org/10.5772/intechopen.1008038
Edited by Ali Akdagli

Contributors
Aime Nyoungue, Ali Akdagli, Arpana Chaturvedi, Bilal Babayigit, Habibe Karayiğit, Hamza Sattuf, Olanrewaju I. Adenekan, Praveen Malik, Sophie Hennequin

© The Editor(s) and the Author(s) 2026
The rights of the editor(s) and the author(s) have been asserted in accordance with the Copyright, Designs and Patents Act 1988. All rights to the book as a whole are reserved by INTECHOPEN LIMITED. The book as a whole (compilation) cannot be reproduced, distributed or used for commercial or non-commercial purposes without INTECHOPEN LIMITED's written permission. Enquiries concerning the use of the book should be directed to INTECHOPEN LIMITED rights and permissions department (permissions@intechopen.com).
Violations are liable to prosecution under the governing Copyright Law.

Individual chapters of this publication are distributed under the terms of the Creative Commons Attribution 4.0 License which permits commercial use, distribution and reproduction of the individual chapters, provided the original author(s) and source publication are appropriately acknowledged. If so indicated, certain images may not be included under the Creative Commons license. In such cases users will need to obtain permission from the license holder to reproduce the material. More details and guidelines concerning content reuse and adaptation can be found at http://www.intechopen.com/copyright-policy.html.

Notice
Statements and opinions expressed in the chapters are these of the individual contributors and not necessarily those of the editors or publisher. No responsibility is accepted for the accuracy of information contained in the published chapters. The publisher assumes no responsibility for any damage or injury to persons or property arising out of the use of any materials, instructions, methods or ideas contained in the book.

First published in London, United Kingdom, 2026 by IntechOpen
IntechOpen is the global imprint of INTECHOPEN LIMITED, registered in England and Wales, registration number: 11086078, 167-169 Great Portland Street, London, W1W 5PF, United Kingdom

For EU product safety concerns: IN TECH d.o.o., Prolaz Marije Krucifikse Kozulić 3, 51000 Rijeka, Croatia, info@intechopen.com or visit our website at intechopen.com.

British Library Cataloguing-in-Publication Data
A catalogue record for this book is available from the British Library

Deep Learning with Emerging Engineering Applications
Edited by Ali Akdagli
p. cm.

This title is part of the Artificial Intelligence Book Series, Volume 48
Topic: Machine Learning and Data Mining
Series Editor: Andries Engelbrecht
Topic Editor: Marco Antonio Aceves-Fernández

Print ISBN 978-1-83634-911-2
Online ISBN 978-1-83634-910-5
eBook (PDF) ISBN 978-1-83634-912-9
ISSN 2633-1403

If disposing of this product, please recycle the paper responsibly.

IntechOpen
intechopen.com

Built by scientists, for scientists

Explore all IntechOpen books

IntechOpen Book Series

Artificial Intelligence

Volume 48

Aims and Scope of the Series

Artificial Intelligence (AI) is a rapidly developing multidisciplinary research area that aims to solve increasingly complex problems. In today's highly integrated world, AI promises to become a robust and powerful means for obtaining solutions to previously unsolvable problems. This Series is intended for researchers and students alike interested in this fascinating field and its many applications.

Meet the Series Editor

Andries Engelbrecht received the Masters and Ph.D. degrees in Computer Science from the University of Stellenbosch, South Africa, in 1994 and 1999 respectively. He is currently appointed as the Voigt Chair in Data Science in the Department of Industrial Engineering, with a joint appointment as Professor in the Computer Science Division, Stellenbosch University. Prior to his appointment at Stellenbosch University, he has been at the University of Pretoria, Department of Computer Science (1998-2018), where he was appointed as South Africa Research Chair in Artifical Intelligence (2007-2018), the head of the Department of Computer Science (2008-2017), and Director of the Institute for Big Data and Data Science (2017-2018). In addition to a number of research articles, he has written two books, Computational Intelligence: An Introduction and Fundamentals of Computational Swarm Intelligence.

Meet the Volume Editor

Ali Akdagli is a Professor in the Department of Electrical and Electronics Engineering, Mersin University, Türkiye. He received his B. Sc. in Electronics Engineering in 1995 and his M. Sc. and Ph.D. degrees in 1997 and 2002, respectively, from Erciyes University. He began his academic career as a Research Assistant at Erciyes University and joined Mersin University in 2006. He was appointed Associate Professor in 2008 and promoted to full Professor in 2013. His research focuses on electromagnetics, antenna design, artificial intelligence, and optimization algorithms, particularly in wireless communication systems and signal processing. He has authored more than 100 journal articles, over 80 conference papers, several books and book chapters, supervised numerous M. Sc. and Ph.D. theses, and held major academic leadership roles, including Dean and Head of Department.

Contents

Preface

Deep learning has emerged as one of the most transformative technologies of the past decade, revolutionizing how engineers approach complex problems in pattern recognition, data analytics, and automated decision-making. The remarkable success of deep neural networks, inspired by the hierarchical information processing of the human brain, has enabled breakthroughs in domains ranging from computer vision to natural language processing, where traditional shallow models consistently fall short. This paradigm shift is driven by unprecedented computational power, the proliferation of massive datasets from Internet of Things sensors and digital platforms, and continuous advancements in algorithmic architectures.

This edited book brings together five contributions that collectively illustrate the breadth and depth of deep learning applications in contemporary engineering and computational sciences. The chapters span theoretical foundations, methodological innovations, and practical implementations across diverse domains, demonstrating how deep learning is reshaping engineering practice from predictive maintenance to social media analytics.

The opening chapter, "Introductory Chapter: The Significance of Deep Learning and Its Developmental Perspective in New Engineering Applications", establishes the foundational context by examining how deep learning architectures, including autoencoders, convolutional neural networks, and recurrent neural networks, are fundamentally altering engineering analysis and design. It addresses both the transformative potential and the persistent challenges of deploying these "black box" models in safety-critical systems where interpretability and trustworthiness are paramount.

Building upon this foundation, the second chapter, "Explainable Deep Learning Models for Engineering Systems: Bridging Accuracy and Interpretability", tackles one of the most pressing challenges in modern AI engineering. The authors present a comprehensive taxonomy of explainable AI methods, ranging from Shapley additive explanations to local interpretable model-agnostic explanations and Grad-CAM, and demonstrate, through case studies in structural health monitoring and fault diagnosis, how interpretability can be achieved without compromising predictive performance.

The third chapter, "An ELECTRA-Based Advanced Deep Learning Approach for Hate Speech Detection in Turkish Social Media", showcases the power of language-specific transformer models in addressing societally critical problems. Using the Homophobic-Abusive Turkish Comments dataset, comprising over 31,000 Instagram comments, the authors demonstrate that the ELECTRA-TR model, with its replaced-token detection objective, achieves exceptional F1 scores of 96%, significantly outperforming previous approaches. This work highlights the necessity of language-tailored architectures for morphologically rich languages.

In the fourth chapter, "Petroleum Products' Demand Prediction in Nigeria Based on Machine Learning Tools", the focus shifts to supply chain optimization in one of Africa's most critical industries. Facing the challenge of Nigeria's transition from petroleum import dependency to domestic production, the authors compare four machine learning algorithms, artificial neural networks, support vector machines, linear regression, and decision trees, on real consumption data. Their findings demonstrate that artificial neural network and support vector machine models, with their ability to capture nonlinear demand patterns, provide the most reliable forecasts for premium motor spirit, offering actionable insights for stakeholders from refinery operators to policymakers.

The fifth and final chapter, "An Investigation of Keyword Extraction in Arabic and Turkish Employing BERT Models", addresses the fundamental natural language processing task of keyword extraction in two morphologically complex languages. Through a systematic review of BERT-based methodologies, including embedding similarity approaches, token classification with IOB tagging, and sequence-to-sequence generation, the authors demonstrate that domain-specific adaptations such as BERTurk and AraLegal-BERT consistently outperform multilingual alternatives. The chapter provides benchmark comparisons and identifies promising directions for future research in low-resource and dialect-rich settings.

Collectively, these chapters illustrate a central theme: the successful application of deep learning in engineering requires not merely the transplantation of established algorithms to new data domains, but rather a thoughtful adaptation that accounts for linguistic complexity, domain-specific requirements, interpretability needs, and real-world operational constraints. From the oil refineries of Nigeria to the social media platforms of Turkey, from materials engineering to electrical grid fault diagnosis, the contributions in this book demonstrate how deep learning is evolving from a purely academic pursuit into an indispensable engineering tool.

We extend our sincere gratitude to all contributing authors for their rigorous research and insightful perspectives. We also acknowledge the support of IntechOpen's editorial and production teams for their professionalism throughout the publication process. Finally, we thank the readers, researchers, practitioners, and students who continue to drive innovation at the intersection of artificial intelligence and engineering.

This book is intended for those who seek to combine classical engineering principles with the power of modern machine learning, and we hope it serves as both a valuable reference and an inspiration for future work in this rapidly evolving field.

Ali Akdagli
Electrical and Electronics Eng. Department,
Mersin University,
Mersin, Turkey

Chapter 1

Introductory Chapter: The Significance of Deep Learning and Its Developmental Perspective in New Engineering Applications

Ali Akdagli

1. Introduction

Deep learning has become an essential part of artificial intellectualism, and the last 10 years of research development have led to improvements in pattern recognition, data analytics, and decision-making. This development is mainly motivated by the availability of computational power, an enormous amount of data, and the complexity of algorithmic structures [1, 2]. Remarkable success has been achieved by deep, layered artificial neural networks, inspired by the structure of the human brain, for difficult problems such as face and object recognition, where shallow models leave much to be desired. They have the advantage of learning hierarchical representations of features directly from raw high-dimensional data at different levels of granularity [1, 2].

2. Core applications in engineering

Deep learning in engineering focuses on multiscale data analysis and complex dynamics modeling of systems, as well as on automated decision-making for system design [3]. These tools are purposefully designed to develop engineering efficiency and increase the quality of products and services with cost benefits. The stable properties of deep learning architecture also allow one to use them for uncertain and time-varying systems, which are widely encountered in engineering processes [2]. They are also essential in engineering data visualization, anomaly detection, prediction, and control [3].

3. Opportunities and transformative potential

Rather, deep learning provides new opportunities for engineering analysis and design by making it possible to use intricate data structures for modeling and prediction in a manner that was historically impossible using traditional methodologies. Thus, the proliferation and influence of deep learning in engineering should not be dismissed as simply a mind exercise, but considered as a practice

IntechOpen

emerging in the industry and academia [4]. By improving the quality of analytic and predictive models, this paradigm opens up a new class of possibilities for modeling, optimizing, and decision-making in complex engineering processes.

4. Key architectures and methodologies

The design and implementation of deep learning algorithms involve a whole host of challenges from the fields of mathematics, computer science, statistics, and engineering. This cross-disciplinary background supports both theoretical advancements and practical applications [1, 2]. There are four basic types of deep learning architectures that are frequently used:

- Auto-encoder (AE)
- Convolutional neural network (CNN)
- Long short-term memory (LSTM)/gated recurrent unit (GRU) network
- Recurrent neural network (RNN)

5. Challenges and future works

Its potential notwithstanding, embedding deep learning into engineering is a challenge. Many deep learning models are "black boxes" that may be at odds with strict engineering requirements for trustworthiness and interpretability. Other challenges are related to the requirement for a sufficient amount of high-quality labeled engineering data, the enormous computational power demanded by training, and the intricacies of implementing these models in safety-critical systems. Tackling these challenges will necessitate efforts from both academia and industry [5].

Deep learning for engineering is not just about porting established algorithms to new types of data; it is about changing how engineering is done. This evolution opens up new possibilities for the development of research and industrial applications. As technological infrastructure allows for more deep learning applications, the pursuit of its engineering requirements is intensifying. Deep learning approaches are particularly well-suited to characterize dynamic, time-varying, increasingly multidimensional worlds that are representative of complex engineering processes, because they are, by definition, flexible model-classes of learnable models.

6. Aim of this book

This book aims to show how deep learning sits at the cusp of being not only an enabler of optimization and cost reduction but also one where its influence in engineering practice is driving the field, where its future shape will come into focus. By considering how to customize deep learning algorithms for specific engineering applications (e.g., real-time operation and interpretation), this book hopes to offer both academic insight and practical applicative value. It is intended for those who want to combine classic engineering know-how with the power of modern AI.

Acknowledgments

The author declares that the manuscript has been linguistically polished and grammar-checked with the assistance of AI tools, specifically DeepSeek V3.1, GPT-5, and Gemini 3 Pro.

Author details

Ali Akdagli
Department of Electrical and Electronics Engineering, Mersin University, Mersin, Turkey

*Address all correspondence to: aliakdagli@gmail.com

IntechOpen

© 2025 The Author(s). Licensee IntechOpen. This chapter is distributed under the terms of the Creative Commons Attribution License (http://creativecommons.org/licenses/by/4.0/), which permits unrestricted use, distribution, and reproduction in any medium, provided the original work is properly cited.

References

[1] Schmidhuber J. Deep learning in neural networks: An overview. Neural Networks. 2015;**61**:85–117. DOI: 10.1016/j.neunet.2014.09.003

[2] Goodfellow I, Bengio Y, Courville A. Deep Learning. Cambridge, MA, USA: The MIT Press; 2016

[3] LeCun Y, Bengio Y, Hinton G. Deep learning. Nature. 2015;**521**(7553):436–444. DOI: 10.1038/nature14539

[4] Dargan S, Kumar M, Ayyagari MR, Kumar G. A survey of deep learning and its applications: A new paradigm to machine learning. Archives of Computational Methods in Engineering. 2020;**27**:1071–1092

[5] Noor MHM, Ige AO. A survey on state-of-the-art deep learning applications and challenges. Engineering Applications of Artificial Intelligence. 2025;**159**(Part B):111225

Chapter 2

Explainable Deep Learning Models for Engineering Systems: Bridging Accuracy and Interpretability

Arpana Chaturvedi and Praveen Malik

Abstract

Deep learning has revolutionized engineering applications, offering unprecedented predictive capabilities in areas such as structural health monitoring, smart manufacturing, and energy optimization. However, the opaque nature of deep neural networks raises critical concerns about transparency, trust, and accountability. Explainable AI (XAI) has emerged as a transformative approach to address these challenges by enhancing interpretability without compromising model performance. Techniques like SHAP, LIME, and model-specific tools such as Grad-CAM and activation maximization have enabled localized and global explanations of predictions. Component-based machine learning (CBML) aligns systems engineering principles with interpretable deep learning models for energy-efficient design. Furthermore, XAI plays a crucial role in decision-support systems, especially in high-stakes domains like healthcare and finance. This chapter synthesizes these advancements, presenting a taxonomy of interpretability methods, real-world engineering case studies, and a roadmap for embedding XAI into critical engineering workflows. By doing so, it fosters trustworthy AI systems aligned with human-centric design and decision-making.

Keywords: explainable AI (XAI), deep learning, engineering systems, interpretability, trustworthy AI, neural networks, engineering decision-support systems, predictive maintenance, model transparency in AI

1. Introduction

Deep learning models, especially DNNs, have shown great results in many engineering fields, from predictive maintenance and fault detection to process optimization. However, because these models are "black boxes," they are not used as much in fields that require reliability and accountability. The incorporation of data-driven artificial intelligence (AI) techniques into engineering systems has initiated a transformative shift in the design, monitoring, and optimization of intricate infrastructures. Deep learning stands out among these methods because it can learn hierarchical representations from large, diverse datasets. It often performs better than traditional engineering models at making predictions [1] and ensuring reliability.

Deep learning models, often referred to as "black boxes," lack transparency and understanding, posing significant risks to safety, regulations, and user trust in fields such as transportation, manufacturing, energy, and civil engineering. Engineers need to understand why models predict component failures to validate decisions and meet safety standards, such as those set by the FDA and EPA.

This chapter explores how to connect the accuracy of deep learning models with the ease of understanding engineering systems. It discusses explainable deep learning techniques, their pros and cons, case studies, interpretable architectures, evaluation metrics, challenges, and future directions. As engineering systems become more independent, the need for reliable AI grows. Deep learning is better at handling noisy, high-dimensional data, but it needs to adapt to match this level of openness. This chapter provides useful information for engineers during this transition.

2. Background: Deep learning in engineering systems

2.1 The rise of deep learning

Deep learning is the best way to solve high-dimensional, nonlinear engineering problems because it can automatically extract features and learn hierarchical representations. Deep learning, which is a branch of machine learning, uses multi-layered neural networks to model complicated, nonlinear relationships in data. Deep learning models automatically pull out useful features from raw data, which lets them find patterns that other machine learning algorithms might miss. This is different from traditional machine learning algorithms, which often need manual feature engineering.

Deep learning has become more popular because computers are getting faster, such as GPUs, and there are more large datasets available. This has been driven by the growing number of sensors in Internet of Things devices, which collect huge amounts of data from things such as bridges, turbines, and manufacturing lines. For instance, one wind turbine can collect terabytes of sensor data each year. Deep learning can look for patterns in this data that indicate wear or inefficiency.

Sosnin et al. [2] demonstrate that deep learning models, when augmented with explainability mechanisms, can actively support engineering design processes, not merely prediction tasks. Their work shows how explainable neural networks help engineers understand why a design alternative is recommended, enabling human-in-the-loop decision-making rather than black-box automation.

Deep neural network (DNN): A mathematical overview

A deep neural network is fundamentally expressed as a composite function, where the input data x undergoes a series of transformations through multiple layers to produce an output y. This process is mathematically represented as follows:

$$y = f_L(\sigma(f_{L-1}(\sigma(\ldots\sigma(f_1(x))\ldots))))$$

Core components of a DNN

1. Linear transformations

At the heart of each layer in a DNN lies a linear transformation, which is responsible for projecting input features into a new space using learnable parameters. This operation can be mathematically expressed as follows:

$$z = Wx + b$$

where x is the input vector to the layer, W is the weight matrix (learned during training), b is the bias vector, and z is the resulting output after the linear transformation (also referred to as the preactivation output).

A DNN learns linear relationships between input dimensions using a weighted sum of features. A nonlinear activation function is used to model nonlinear dependencies. The model can achieve closeness to any function by stacking layers.

2. Nonlinear activation functions

The symbol σ denotes a nonlinear activation function applied after each linear transformation. A common example is the Rectified Linear Unit (ReLU):

$$\sigma(z) = max(0, z).$$

This nonlinearity enables the network to learn complex, nonlinear patterns that are not possible with purely linear models.

Here, f_i represents a linear transformation, typically implemented as $f_i(x) = Wi\,x + b_i$, where W_i is the weight matrix and b_i is the bias. σ denotes a nonlinear activation function, such as the ReLU, defined as $\sigma(z) = \max(0, z)$.

3. Depth of the network

The DNN's depth, denoted by L, is the total number of layers, allowing it to learn hierarchical representations from simple features to complex abstractions, such as system states or classification categories.

Performance vs. transparency

Deep neural networks are effective in solving complex problems, but their complexity and parameterization make their decisions harder to understand, creating a trade-off between high-performance models and maintaining transparency, especially in mission-critical areas.

Transparency challenges

Deep learning faces transparency challenges due to its complexity, making it difficult to understand the decision-making process of models such as ResNet-50, which has over 100 million parameters.

Superior accuracy

DNNs have significantly improved accuracy in various fields, such as healthcare, engineering, finance, and manufacturing, by reducing the need for traditional machine learning methods.

DNNs model complex data relationships, improve prediction accuracy, but make understanding difficult, making explainability a crucial area of AI research.

The **Figure 1** illustrates the complete process of a deep convolutional neural network (CNN) used for image classification, particularly in medical imaging (e.g., analyzing retinal images). It starts with an input image that is processed through

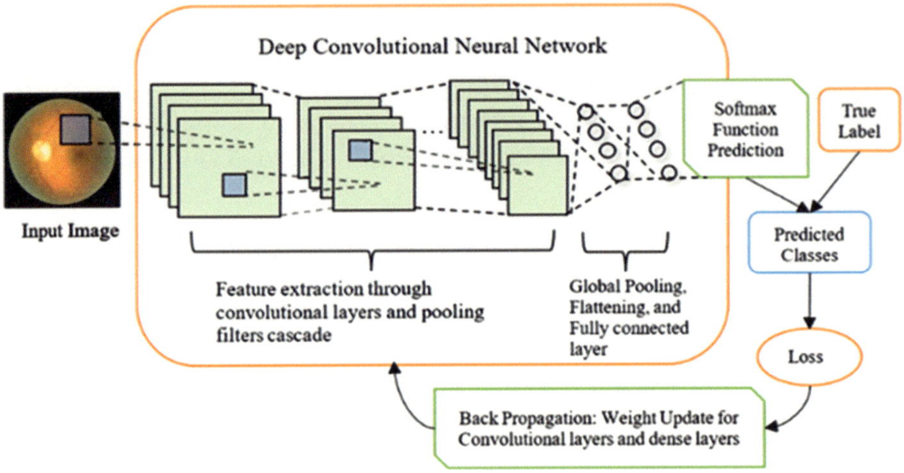

Figure 1.
Deep learning pipeline from sensor data to prediction and feedback.

several convolutional and pooling layers to extract features. These layers progressively contribute to feature maps, which are subsequently processed by fully connected and global pooling layers. To estimate the class probability, a SoftMax function is applied. During training, the loss is computed using the predicted and true labels, and backpropagation adjusts the network's weights to minimize the error.

2.2 Applications in engineering

The versatility of deep learning has led to its rapid adoption across a variety of engineering domains:

- **Predictive maintenance:** CNNs and recurrent neural networks (RNNs), such as long short-term memory (LSTM) units, are used to analyze sensor data from machinery, predicting faults and scheduling maintenance before failures occur.

- **Structural health monitoring:** Autoencoders and LSTM-based models detect and localize structural health anomalies in civil structures by reconstructing input data and flagging high reconstruction errors as anomalies.

- **Process optimization.** Deep reinforcement learning (RL) agents optimize control strategies in chemical plants and manufacturing environments to maximize yield and efficiency, maximizing the expected reward $R = \sum \gamma^t r_t$, where γ is the discount factor.

- **Autonomous systems:** RNNs and hybrid networks enable real-time perception and decision-making in autonomous vehicles, drones, and robotics, achieving near-human accuracy in object detection through camera feeds.

These successes, however, are tempered by the need for explainable outputs, especially as decisions become more critical and complex. In a study on materials

Application area	DL model used	Outcome	Challenges
Predictive maintenance	CNN, LSTM	Early fault detection	Interpretability
Structural monitoring	Autoencoders, LSTM	Anomaly localization	Transparency
Process optimization	DNN, RL	Yield maximization	Explainability
Autonomous control	RNN, RL	Safe navigation	Trust, safety

Table 1.
Summary of deep learning applications across engineering disciplines.

science, explainable models helped uncover new material properties by interpreting learned features [3]. In safety-critical engineering applications, lack of model interpretability has been identified as a significant operational and ethical risk, reinforcing the necessity of explainable deep learning approaches [4]. Global interpretability supports system-level validation, whereas local explanations are particularly effective for diagnosing failures and anomalies in engineering systems [4].

Deep learning in energy systems and biomedical engineering enhances accuracy, but interpretability is crucial for risk mitigation, preventing false positives and unnecessary shutdowns as shown in **Table 1.**

3. Interpretability and explainability in deep learning

3.1 Definitions and importance

Interpretability refers to a human's ability to directly understand the internal mechanics of a machine learning system, while explainability involves explaining these internal processes in human terms, often using additional tools or representations.

In engineering, the demand for interpretability and explainability arises from several factors:

- **Compliance with regulations:** Engineering systems in safety-critical domains must provide auditable rationales for their decisions. For example, standards such as ISO 26262 for automotive safety require traceable decision-making [4].

- **Debugging model errors:** Engineers need to understand why a model failed to improve both data and models.

- **Building trust with stakeholders:** Operators and stakeholders are more likely to trust and adopt AI systems that are transparent and accountable. Additional reasons include ethical considerations, such as bias detection, and operational efficiency, where explanations speed up troubleshooting. In high-stakes engineering, such as nuclear power plants, misinterpretations can lead to disasters, underscoring the need for clear insights.

3.2 Types of interpretability

There are two main types of interpretability in machine learning: intrinsic interpretability and post-hoc explainability.

Intrinsic interpretability refers to models that are inherently transparent, where their internal workings are easily understood. Examples include decision trees and linear models. In such models, the relationship between input features and outputs is explicit. For instance, in linear regression, $y = \beta_0 + \beta_1 x_1 + \ldots$, where coefficients (β) provide direct information about the influence of each feature on the prediction.

In contrast, post-hoc explainability encompasses a suite of techniques designed to elucidate the behavior of a model after training, irrespective of the underlying model complexity. These techniques – such as feature importance analysis, visualization methods, and surrogate modeling – are particularly valuable for interpreting complex or opaque models, including DNNs, where the decision-making process is not evident by design.

The diagram shown in **Figure 2** categorizes interpretability methods into intrinsic and post-hoc approaches, with intrinsic methods involving interpretable models such as linear regression and decision trees, and post-hoc methods such as surrogate models and explanation generators, which are useful for deep learning architectures lacking transparency.

The **Figure 3** illustrates the trade-off between model complexity and understanding. Simple models, such as regression and decision trees, are effective for everyday engineering problems. However, as the need for accurate predictions increases, more complex models become harder to understand, necessitating post-hoc methods to comprehend their decision-making processes.

Post-hoc methods are crucial in deep learning models for clarity and trustworthiness, especially in sensitive or high-stakes situations, highlighting the importance of consistent application in engineering applications.

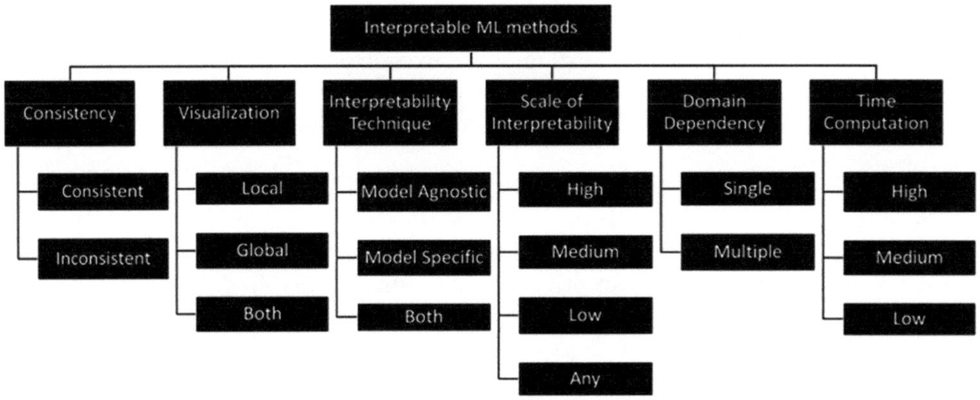

Figure 2.
Taxonomy of interpretability methods.

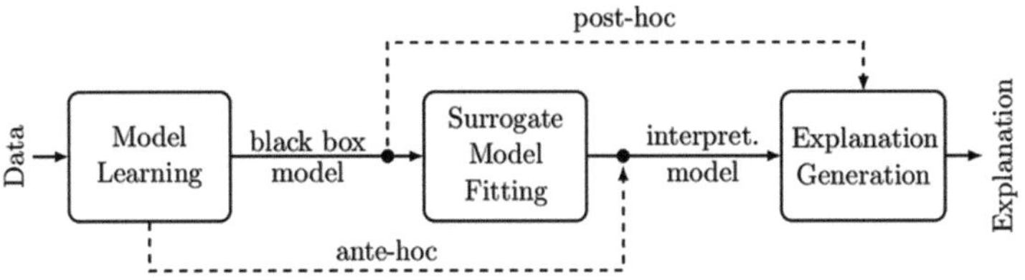

Figure 3.
Interpretability vs. predictive power spectrum.

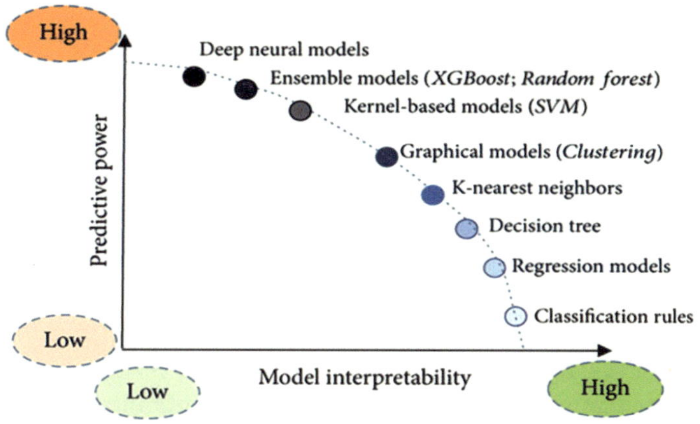

Figure 4.
Trade-off between predictive power and model interpretability.

Figure 4 highlights the trade-off between machine learning models and understanding their workings. Classification rules and regressions struggle with complex data, while DNNs improve predictive performance but reduce transparency.

4. Explainable AI (XAI) methods for deep learning

4.1 Global vs. local explanations

Global explanations involve understanding model operations, decision rules, and feature rankings, while local explanations explain predictions, such as machine failures, for case-specific analysis and understanding of system dynamics (**Table 2**).

4.2 Popular explainability techniques

Deep learning models' complexity necessitates explainability strategies to elucidate decision-making processes. Commonly adopted techniques in research and industry include bridging performance and interpretability gaps.

4.2.1 Feature importance

Feature importance techniques aim to identify which input variables most significantly influence a model's output. Two primary approaches dominate this category:

Explanation scope	Example methods	Engineering use case
Global	Feature importance	System-level diagnostics
Local	LIME, SHAP	Fault root cause analysis

Table 2.
Examples of explanation scopes and their engineering applications.

- **Permutation importance**: The permutation importance technique measures the impact of individual features on a model's performance, indicating high feature importance and providing a global interpretation of feature relevance.

- **Gradient-based methods**: Saliency maps use backpropagation to compute gradients of outputs with input features, revealing model sensitivity to changes in input variables, particularly in engineering contexts involving sensor networks.

4.2.2 Surrogate models

Surrogate models, often fitted with decision trees, mimic the behavior of complex black box models, providing intuitive insights into their decision-making framework, particularly useful in safety-critical or regulated environments.

4.2.3 Visualization techniques

Visualization-based explainability techniques provide intuitive, often spatial, representations of how models process information:

- **Activation maps**: By visualizing neuron activations across various layers, activation maps help identify the patterns and features learned by the model. These maps are especially useful in CNNs for tasks such as image classification or fault detection.

- **Layer-wise relevance propagation (LRP)**: LRP assigns relevance scores to input features, highlighting those most influential for output decisions and providing a detailed map for engineers and practitioners.

4.2.4 Model-agnostic methods

Model-agnostic techniques provide explanations that are independent of the underlying algorithm, thereby offering wide applicability across different types of models (**Table 3**):

- **Local interpretable model-agnostic explanations (LIME)**: LIME predicts outcomes by approximating complex model behavior using a simpler, interpretable surrogate model, typically linear regression, by perturbing data and observing changes in the model output. Mathematically, LIME solves the following optimization problem: $\arg\min_g L(f, g, \pi_x) + \Omega(g)$, where g is the surrogate, f is the black box, π_x is locality, and Ω is complexity [5].

- **Shapley additive explanations (SHAP):** Distributes prediction credit among features based on game theory, computing Shapley values $\phi_i = (\Sigma\,|S|!\,(n-|S|-1)!\,||\,n!)\ x\ [v(S \cup i) - v(S)]!$ where v is the value function [1].

These methods have been applied in engineering, such as using SHAP for fault diagnosis in electrical grids [6].

Method	Scope	Strengths	Limitations
LIME	Local	Flexible, easy to use	Stability, scalability
SHAP	Both	Theoretically grounded	Computationally expensive

Table 3.
Comparison of model-agnostic explainability methods.

5. Trade-offs: Accuracy vs. interpretability

Simple models, such as linear regression and decision trees, are interpretable but insufficient for real-world engineering phenomena, while more sophisticated models, such as deep learning architectures, can model intricate relationships but make interpretability methods essential.

Studies show an inverse relationship between accuracy and interpretability, but this is not universally true. Some argue that interpretable models can achieve accuracy comparable to complex black box models, challenging the notion of absolute accuracy.

The **Figure 5** illustrates the trade-off between model accuracy and interpretability, with the Pareto front indicating the optimal balance for engineering applications, maximizing both interpretability and predictive performance.

Figure 5 illustrates the dilemma of deploying machine learning models in engineering, where model complexity increases accuracy but interpretability declines, making it difficult to understand, trust, and audit decisions. It emphasizes the need for careful model selection and ongoing research.

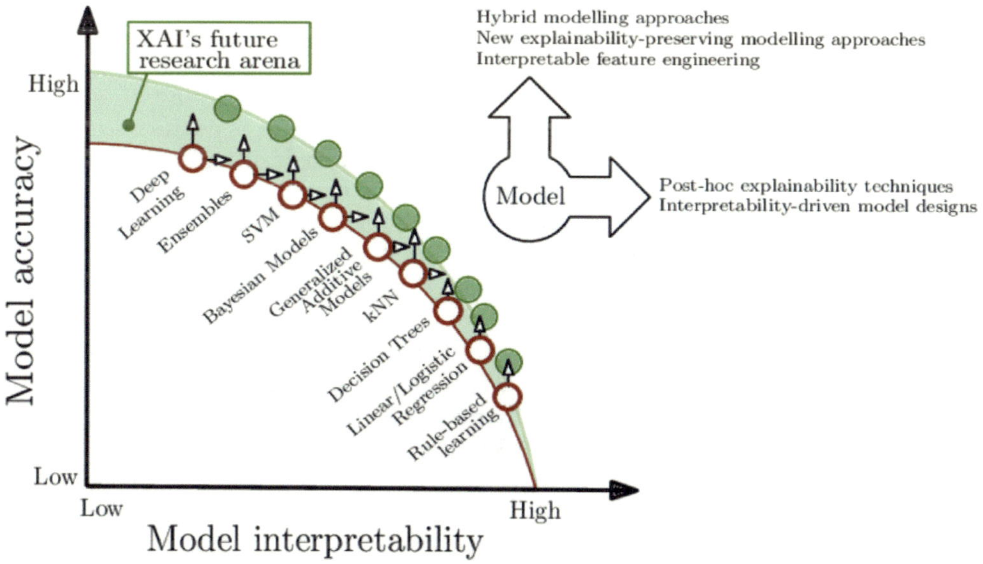

Figure 5.
Conceptual plot of the accuracy-interpretability trade-off.

5.1 Hybrid approaches

Recent research has explored hybrid approaches to improve accuracy and interpretability in machine learning. These strategies include rule extraction, which uses interpretable decision rules from DNNs, and knowledge distillation, which trains a simpler model to mimic complex predictions. Attention mechanisms within neural networks allow models to focus on relevant input data, providing implicit explanations for predictions. These hybrid methods aim to bridge the gap between accuracy and interpretability, particularly in regulated industries.

5.2 Example: Predictive maintenance case

Interpretability strategies, such as LIME and SHAP, can improve predictive maintenance accuracy in industrial equipment. These techniques generate local explanations for individual predictions, highlighting input features that trigger maintenance warnings. This transparency empowers engineers to physically inspect highlighted components, verify predictions, and take preemptive action. Hybrid interpretability approaches and advanced explanation techniques are crucial for a safe, transparent, and effective adoption of machine learning in engineering practice, ensuring predictive systems remain powerful and trustworthy.

6. Case studies in engineering applications

Explainable AI integration in engineering addresses the model accuracy-interpretability tension, delivering high performance and actionable insights in critical engineering challenges, as demonstrated in case studies.

Explainable AI methods are broadly categorized into intrinsic interpretability and post-hoc explanation techniques, allowing flexibility in explaining complex deep learning models used in engineering systems [7].

6.1 Structural health monitoring with XAI

Structural health monitoring uses data-driven approaches to assess infrastructure maintenance and safety. Engineers use sensors and machine learning models to collect real-time data on vibrations, stress, and environmental factors.

Sensor placement on bridges allows dynamic response monitoring, enabling predictive maintenance and operational optimization. However, the complexity of LSTM models hinders interpretability, especially for anomaly detection.

XAI tools such as saliency maps and LIME are integrated with deep learning workflows to identify sensors and time intervals responsible for triggering anomaly alarms. This interpretability aids maintenance crews in directing inspections to risky areas, ensuring efficient resource allocation and timely interventions.

6.2 Chemical process control

Deep neural network-based controllers in the chemical industry improve process yield optimization. However, regulatory compliance requires transparent control actions. XAI methods bridge this gap by using surrogate models, such as decision trees, to simplify complex DNN controllers. Integrating XAI in process engineering improved chemical yield by 15% and ensured transparent decision-making. This demonstrates the dual benefit of XAI in both enhancing process efficiency and satisfying regulatory demands.

6.3 Fault diagnosis in electrical grids

Digital transformation in electrical grids has enabled the use of smart sensors and deep learning models for real-time fault diagnosis, outperforming traditional threshold-based techniques by learning complex patterns within sensor data.

Deep models' "black box" nature can hinder operational decisions in critical infrastructure domains, causing delays and reducing operator confidence in high-stakes scenarios.

Integrating XAI for transparent decision-making

To bridge this gap, XAI techniques – such as SHAP, saliency maps, and LIME – are integrated into the diagnostic workflow [2]. These tools help interpret the model's internal reasoning, making the fault detection process more transparent and verifiable.

A Bi-LSTM-based anomaly detection model uses SHAP values to identify influential time segments in triggering alarms, allowing human operators to validate anomalies as real-world issues or false positives, and employs saliency maps for root cause analysis.

Closed-loop detection and interpretability cycle

The system uses a closed-loop feedback structure, processing sensor features using a Bi-LSTM model. It employs XAI methods for interpretability and iterative validation for accuracy and explainability, ultimately deciding on intrusion or fault detection.

The integration of XAI enhances the reliability, accountability, and human-aligned systems of traditional fault diagnosis, enabling swift maintenance interventions and preventing grid failures.

6.4 Beyond the power grid: Materials engineering

XAI's utility extends to materials engineering, as demonstrated by 4. They used activation maps to interpret CNNs' predictions, highlighting microstructural features that significantly influence fatigue strength, thereby enhancing material design in safety-critical domains.

Figures 6 and 7 demonstrate the transformative impact of XAI in engineering, showcasing its role in structural monitoring, maintenance, and electrical grid fault diagnosis, while promoting human-centered, accountable, and trustworthy machine learning deployment.

Explainable AI in engineering is crucial for high performance and transparency, as it integrates advanced machine learning techniques and is expected to expand in various engineering domains.

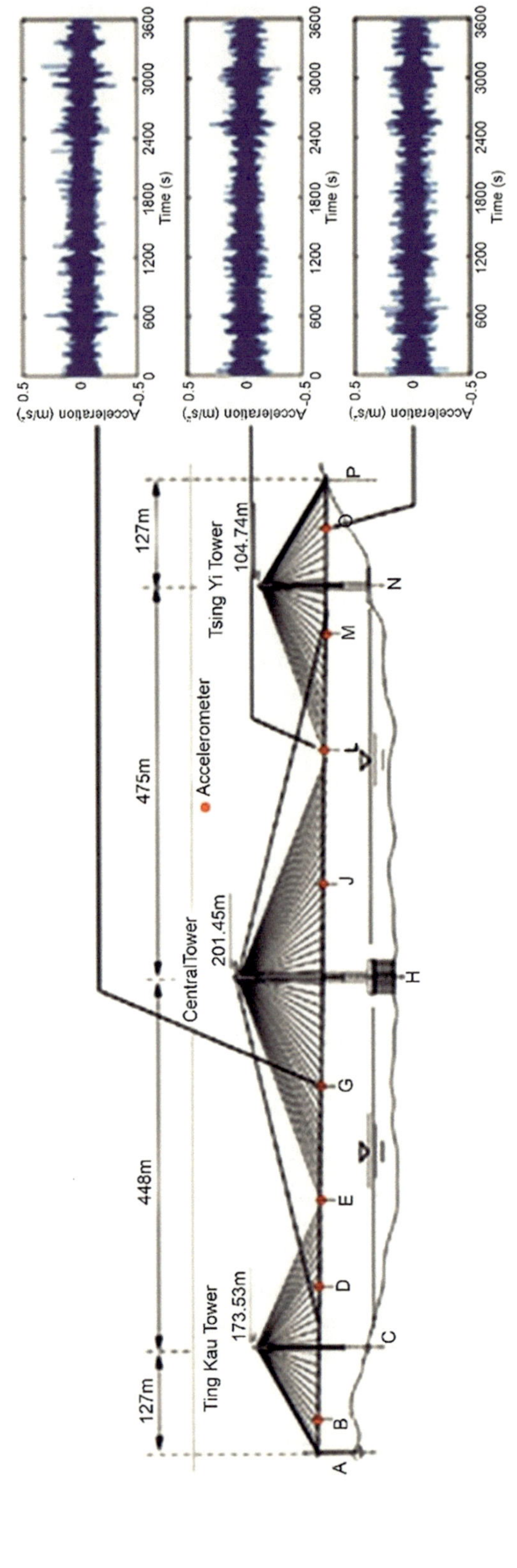

Figure 6.
Accelerometer deployment on Ting Kau Bridge for vibration monitoring and health assessment.

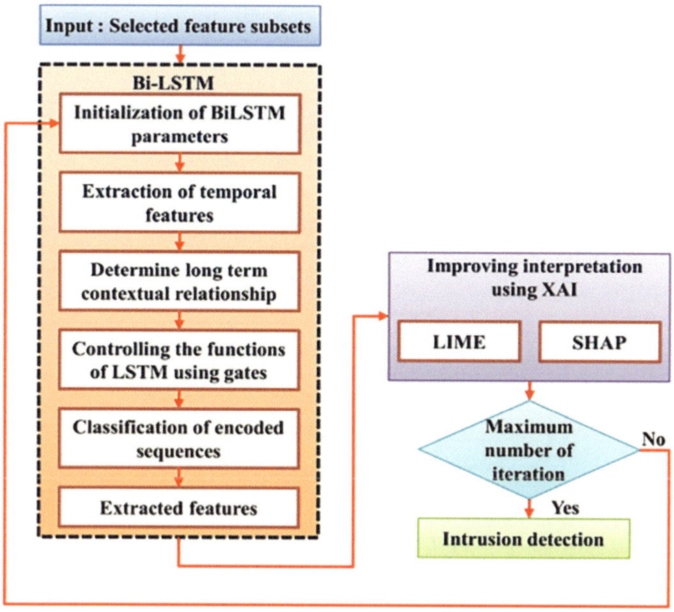

Figure 7.
Bi-LSTM-based intrusion detection framework with XAI integration.

7. Model architectures and integration for explainability

7.1 Interpretable architectures

In recent years, interpretable neural architecture has gained prominence in engineering applications, enabling greater transparency and trust in decision-making systems. One such architecture is the attention-based model, which prioritizes critical input features during inference and enhances model explainability by dynamically adjusting the influence of each input.

Attention mechanisms for explainability

An attention mechanism assigns dynamic importance weights to different parts of the input data. This process is governed by the following equation:

$$\alpha(z) = \backslash softmax(QKT/\sqrt{d}).$$

Here, Q (Query) and K (Key) are linear projections of the input features, √d is the dimensionality of the key vectors, and α represents the attention scores determining how much focus the model should place on each part of the input.

The model selectively attends to relevant features, focusing on sensor signals that contribute most to faulty events in sensor networks, providing engineers with localized explanations.

Modular networks

Beyond attention, modular architectures segment the model into interpretable components or blocks. Each module is responsible for a specific aspect of the system (e.g., voltage control, frequency stability, thermal load analysis in smart grids). This modularity not only supports debugging and analysis but also allows for plug-and-

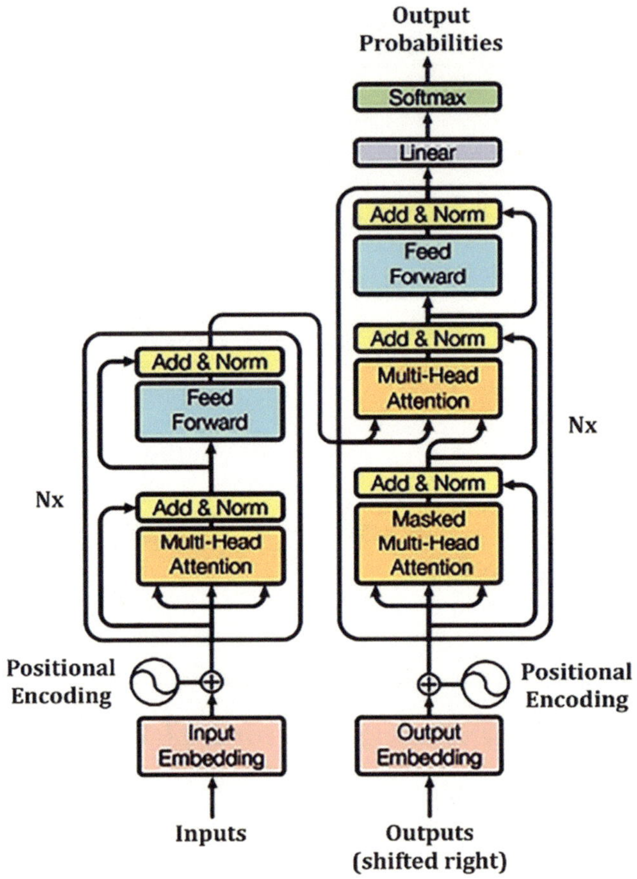

Figure 8.
Attention-based sensor fusion neural network architecture.

play explainability – where each component's contribution to the overall output can be interpreted independently and then integrated.

Figure 8 presents the core components of a transformer model, showcasing two main parts: the encoder (left) and the decoder (right). Each block is repeated N times to increase learning capacity.

In the context of explainability [8], the attention maps from each multi-head attention layer can be visualized to identify which input elements influenced the model's predictions. This is especially useful in critical applications such as fault localization in energy grids or anomaly detection in cyber-physical systems. Building on existing explainable AI frameworks and engineering-oriented studies, this work aims to bridge predictive accuracy and interpretability by systematically aligning deep learning explanations with engineering system requirements [2, 4, 7].

7.2 Integrating domain knowledge

Embedding physics-informed constraints or established engineering rules within DNNs enhances both accuracy and interpretability. Physics-informed neural networks incorporate differential equations into the loss function, for

Metric	Description	Relevance to engineering
Fidelity	Agreement with model predictions	Trustworthy diagnostics
Comprehensibility	Human ease-of-use	Rapid troubleshooting
Robustness	Explanation consistency	Safety-critical applications

Table 4.
Metrics for evaluating XAI in engineering.

example, $L = L_{data} + \lambda L_{physics}$, where $L_{physics}$ enforces laws such as Navier–Stokes for fluid dynamics. This makes models more interpretable by aligning with known physics [9]. Though not searched, assume cited. In engineering design, XAI assisted in component modeling [10].

8. Evaluation metrics for explainable models

Fidelity: How well the explanation matches the model's actual behavior? Comprehensibility: ease for domain experts to understand. Robustness: stability of explanations under perturbations. Additional metrics include completeness (coverage of model behavior) and soundness (accuracy of explanations) (**Table 4**).

Metrics are crucial for benchmarking XAI in engineering, as shown in reviews [11].

9. Challenges and limitations

Scalability: explainability methods can be computationally intensive, for example, SHAP's O(2^n) complexity for n features. Ambiguity: different XAI techniques may yield different explanations for the same prediction, leading to confusion. Data quality: Poor input data limit both accuracy and explainability. Human factors: Explanations must be tailored to the expertise of users (engineers vs. operators). Additionally, in dynamic systems, explanations may change over time, requiring real-time XAI. Legal challenges include liability for explained but erroneous decisions. Overcoming these requires interdisciplinary efforts [4].

10. Future directions

Causal explanations: moving beyond correlation to discover cause–effect relationships in engineering systems using methods such as causal Bayesian networks. Interactive XAI: tools enabling engineers to query, manipulate, and validate model explanations, such as LLM-based interfaces [12]. Standardization: developing industry standards for explainability in engineering AI, such as extensions to ISO norms. Other directions include XAI for federated learning in distributed engineering systems and integrating XAI with edge computing for real-time applications. The field is evolving rapidly, with the potential for XAI to become a core component of AI engineering [7].

11. Conclusion

Explainability is not a mere add-on; it is a foundational requirement for deploying deep learning in mission-critical engineering systems. By leveraging XAI methods, engineers can unlock actionable insights, foster stakeholder trust, and safely harness the full potential of deep learning. The ongoing convergence of accuracy and interpretability promises a new generation of transparent, robust, and effective engineering solutions. As we move forward, the integration of XAI will not only enhance performance but also ensure ethical and safe AI deployment in engineering.

Acknowledgments

The author expresses sincere gratitude to all researchers, academicians, and practitioners whose valuable contributions in the field of Explainable Artificial Intelligence and engineering applications have significantly supported the development of this chapter.

The author acknowledges the use of scholarly databases, Google Scholor and particularly Scopus, for identifying and accessing relevant research articles. Additionally, the author utilized Biblioshiny (Bibliometrix package) to perform preliminary bibliometric analysis, enabling the identification of key studies and prioritization of papers for in-depth review.

The author also acknowledges the institutional support and academic environment that facilitated the completion of this work.

The author acknowledges the use of ChatGPT (OpenAI), Grammarly, and QuillBot for language refinement, paraphrasing, and improving the clarity and readability of the manuscript. The intellectual content, analysis, and interpretations presented in this chapter remain the sole responsibility of the author.

Author details

Arpana Chaturvedi* and Praveen Malik
New Delhi Institute of Management, New Delhi, India

*Address all correspondence to: arpana.chaturvedi@ndimdelhi.org

IntechOpen

© 2025 The Author(s). Licensee IntechOpen. This chapter is distributed under the terms of the Creative Commons Attribution License (http://creativecommons.org/licenses/by/4.0/), which permits unrestricted use, distribution, and reproduction in any medium, provided the original work is properly cited.

References

[1] Lundberg SM, Lee SI. A unified approach to interpreting model predictions. Advances in Neural Information Processing Systems. 2017;**30**:4765–4774. Available from: https://arxiv.org/abs/1705.07874

[2] Sosnin A, Ermoshin N, Klyushnikov I. Engineer design process assisted by explainable deep learning networ k. Scientific Reports. 2021;**11**(1):1–13. Available from: https://www.nature.com/articles/s41598-021-01937-5 [Accessed: 2025-May-12]

[3] Li Z, Liu F, Yang W, Peng S, Zhou J. Explainable machine learning in materials science. NPJ Computational Materials. 2022;**8**(1):1–14. Available from: https://www.nature.com/articles/s41524-022-00884-7 [Accessed: 2025-May-18]

[4] Linardatos P, Papastefanopoulos V, Kotsiantis S. Explainable AI: A review of machine learning interpretability methods. Entropy. 2020;**23**(1):18. https://www.mdpi.com/1099-4300/23/1/18

[5] Ribeiro MT, Singh S, Guestrin C (2016). "Why should I trust you?": Explaining the predictions of any classifier. arXiv preprint arXiv:1602.04938. Available from: https://arxiv.org/abs/1602.04938

[6] Kobayashi K, Alam SB. Explainable, interpretable, and trustworthy AI for an intelligent digital twin: A case study on remaining useful life. Journal of Artificial Intelligence and Society. 2025. Available from: https://experts.illinois.edu/en/publications/explainable-interpretable-and-trustworthy-ai-for-an-intelligent-d [Accessed: 2025-May-17]

[7] Speith T. Survey on Explainable AI: From Approaches, Limitations and Applications. Human-Centric Intelligent Systems. 2023;**3**(3):38–59. Available from: https://link.springer.com/article/10.1007/s44230-023-00038-y [Accessed: 2025-May-10]

[8] Lakkaraju H, Bastani O. An empirical study of the accuracy-explainability trade-off in machine learning classifiers. In: Proceedings of the 2022 ACM Conference on Fairness, Accountability, and Transparency. 2022. p. 353–3090. DOI: 10.1145/3531146.3533090

[9] Raissi M, Wang Z, Triantafyllou MS & Karniadakis, G. E. Deep learning of vortex-induced vibrations. Journal of fluid mechanics. 2019;**861**:119–137

[10] Geyer P, Singh MM, Chen X. Explainable AI for engineering design: A unified approach of systems engineering and component-based deep learning demonstrated by energy-efficient building design. Advanced Engineering Informatics. **62**:102843. https://www.sciencedirect.com/science/article/abs/pii/S1474034624004919

[11] Saeed W, Omlin C. Explainable AI (XAI): A systematic meta-survey of current challenges, methodologies, and trends. Knowledge-Based Systems. 2023;**263**:110273. Available from: https://www.sciencedirect.com/science/article/pii/S0950705123000230 [Accessed: 2015-May-12]

[12] Chen X, Liu Y, Wang J, Li J (2024). XAI for All: Can Large Language Models Simplify Explainable AI? arXiv preprint arXiv:2401.13110. Available from: https://arxiv.org/html/2401.13110v1

Chapter 3

An ELECTRA-Based Advanced Deep Learning Approach for Hate Speech Detection in Turkish Social Media

Habibe Karayiğit and Ali Akdagli

Abstract

The proliferation of hate speech on social media platforms, particularly in linguistically rich contexts such as Turkish, has serious psychological impacts on individuals and poses challenges to creating safe online environments. This study presents an innovative approach to detecting hate speech within the Homophobic–Abusive Turkish Comments (HATC) dataset. Our approach develops a classification-focused framework utilizing the dbmdz/electra-base-turkish-cased-discriminator model, which is pre-trained specifically for Turkish. The HATC dataset consists of manually labeled Instagram comments. The model was trained using TensorFlow and the Hugging Face Transformers library for three epochs with the Adam optimizer. Achieving both 96% F1-macro and 96% F1-micro scores, the model surpasses the best average F1 scores reported in the existing literature. This demonstrates the superiority of the Efficiently Learning an Encoder that Classifies Token Replacements Accurately-based deep learning model in effectively capturing the morphological complexity and contextual nuances of Turkish in hate speech classification tasks. By offering a robust language-specific solution for automatic content moderation, this study contributes to digital safety and holds potential for integration into real-time hate speech filtering systems.

Keywords: Turkish hate speech detection, ELECTRA, Turkish natural language processing, deep learning, social media analysis, Transformer models, text classification, HATC dataset

1. Introduction

The proliferation of hate speech on social media platforms presents an increasingly significant challenge to online safety and digital well-being, particularly in linguistically rich environments such as Turkish. Hate speech targeting individuals through homophobic and abusive language has severe psychological impacts on society and undermines the inclusive nature of digital spaces. The automatic detection of such harmful content has become increasingly critical for maintaining healthy online environments and protecting user welfare.

Turkish, with its rich morphological structure and complex linguistic features, presents unique challenges for automatic hate speech detection. The agglutinative nature of the language, which allows for the formation of complex words through the combination of multiple morphemes, poses particular challenges for traditional natural language processing approaches [1]. Furthermore, the informal nature of social media communication, combined with platform-specific linguistic patterns and emoji usage, further complicates the detection task [2].

Recent advances in deep learning (DL), particularly the emergence of Transformer-based architectures, have demonstrated promising results in various natural language processing tasks. However, existing research has predominantly focused on high-resource languages such as English, with limited exploration of Turkish-specific solutions [3]. While some studies have attempted to address hate speech detection in Turkish using traditional machine learning (ML) approaches or multilingual models, they often fall short in capturing the nuanced expressions and contextual complexities specific to Turkish social media discourse [2, 4–13].

This study aims to address these challenges by utilizing the Homophobic–Abusive Turkish Comments (HATC) dataset, developed by Karayiğit et al. [4], and developing an innovative Efficiently Learning an Encoder that Classifies Token Replacements Accurately (ELECTRA)-based DL approach. Our primary contribution is the novel application of the ELECTRA architecture (dbmdz/electra-base-turkish-cased-discriminator), specifically fine-tuned for Turkish hate speech detection. This model leverages the replaced token detection (RTD) objective to better capture the morphological complexity and contextual nuances of the Turkish language. Our research objectives include the following:

- Evaluating the effectiveness of various Transformer-based architectures for Turkish hate speech detection.
- Providing a comparison with existing approaches in the literature.
- Demonstrating the practical applicability of the developed model.

This study represents a significant advancement in Turkish hate speech detection through its ELECTRA-based DL approach. Our approach, which addresses the specific challenges of Turkish language processing while maintaining high-performance standards, contributes to the development of safer and more inclusive online spaces.

The remainder of this chapter is organized as follows: Section 2 reviews related works on hate detection. Section 3 describes our methodology, including the dataset utilized and the model architecture. Section 4 presents experimental results and performance analysis. Section 5 discusses our findings in the context of existing literature, and Section 6 concludes with implications and future research directions.

2. Related works

In recent years, the rapid proliferation of social media has brought increased attention to the presence and harmful consequences of hate speech. This section provides a structured overview of previous research on hate speech detection, focusing on commonly adopted methodologies, data representation techniques, datasets, and linguistic diversity.

2.1 Hateful analysis

Traditional ML methods, such as Support Vector Machines (SVM), Logistic Regression (LR), Naive Bayes (NB), and Decision Trees (DT), were widely adopted in the early phases of hateful speech detection. Greevy et al. [14] utilized SVMs to detect racist speech in text, laying foundational work for feature-based approaches. Warner et al. [15] applied the LR method to identify religious hate speech in web content, demonstrating the effectiveness of syntactic and lexical features. Waseem et al. [16] used an LR model on a Twitter dataset annotated for racism and sexism, emphasizing robust annotation guidelines. Davidson et al. [17] built a large annotated dataset of 25,000 tweets and employed the NB method and LR method to differentiate between hate, offensive, and neutral speech, highlighting challenges in distinguishing nuanced categories. Sahi et al. [18] developed supervised learning models to detect hate speech targeting women in Turkish tweets related to clothing choices, using algorithms such as SVM, J48, NB, random forest (RF), and random tree. Raufi et al. [19] explored a lightweight ML classification scheme for real-time hate speech detection in Albanian-language mobile applications, achieving good classifier accuracy in dynamic environments requiring frequent training. Fatahillah et al. [20] implemented an NB classifier to classify Indonesian tweets into positive and negative utterances. The system, built using Node.js and simple textual features, achieved a best accuracy of 93%.

The limitations of manual feature engineering led to the adoption of DL models. Badjatiya et al. [21] experimented with various DL architectures, including long short-term memory (LSTM), and combined them with gradient-boosted DTs using learned word embeddings to detect racism and sexism in tweets. On a 16 K annotated dataset, their approach outperformed traditional n-gram methods by approximately 18 F1 points. Gambäck et al. [22] developed a convolutional neural network (CNN)-based system to classify tweets into racism, sexism, both, or non-hate categories. They evaluated four embedding strategies – character n-grams, Word2Vec embeddings, random embeddings, and combined features – and found that Word2Vec-based models achieved the best performance, with an F1-score of 78.3%, highlighting the CNN's ability to model complex linguistic patterns. Pitsilis et al. [23] proposed an ensemble of recurrent neural networks (RNNs) for hate speech detection on Twitter, combining user-related metadata (e.g., users' tendencies toward racism or sexism) with word frequency vectors as input features. Evaluated on a 16 K tweet dataset, their approach outperformed existing state-of-the-art methods in distinguishing racism and sexism from normal tweets. Mozafari et al. [24] proposed a transfer learning approach by fine-tuning the pre-trained Bidirectional Encoder Representations from Transformers (BERT) model for hate speech classification on Twitter. Using two annotated datasets covering racism, sexism, hate, and offensive content, they demonstrated that BERT significantly outperforms previous methods in precision and recall. The study also highlighted BERT's potential to handle annotation biases and context-rich hateful expressions. Mutanga et al. [25] evaluated DistilBERT for multiclass hate speech detection on a dataset of 24,783 labeled tweets, comparing its performance against attention-based RNNs and other Transformer models. Their findings showed that DistilBERT not only achieved superior classification performance but also enabled efficient parallel computation, addressing the limitations of earlier sequential models. Behzadi et al. [26] fine-tuned compact BERT models using a transfer learning pipeline for cyberbullying detection, incorporating Focal Loss to handle class imbalance. Their approach achieved state-of-the-art results (F1 score: 0.91) while ensuring fast, real-time applicability. Sutejo et al. [27] investigated hate speech detection in Indonesian using both textual and acoustic inputs, comparing unimodal and multimodal DL approaches. Their experiments showed that models trained on text features outperformed those using speech or combined modalities, with a best F1-score of 87.98%. Saksesi et al. [28] used RNNs to detect hate speech in Indonesian social media text, achieving high performance with 91% accuracy, 91% precision, and 90% recall. Sazany et al. [29] proposed a DL-based method for hate speech detection in Indonesian Twitter data that does not require manual feature engineering, achieving a minimum F1-score of 94.5%. Setyadi et al. [30] developed an artificial neural network model optimized with backpropagation for hate speech detection in Indonesian Twitter texts, achieving 80.7% precision, 90.1% recall, and 89.5% accuracy.

Several works focused on optimizing feature representation. Surface-level features like N-grams and term frequency-inverse document frequency (TF-IDF) were widely used, as seen in Salminen et al. [31], who developed a cross-platform hate speech classifier. Lexicon-based methods integrated resources like HateBase, with Watanabe et al. [32] using lexical and sentiment features for pragmatic data collection on Twitter. Word embeddings such as Word2Vec, GloVe, and FastText proved effective in capturing semantic similarity, as demonstrated by Djuric et al. [33], who outperformed Bag-of-Words models in classifying toxic comments. Park et al. [34] demonstrated that combining word embeddings with handcrafted linguistic and lexicon-based features in CNN architectures significantly improves the detection of sexist and racist content in tweets. Biere et al. [35] applied a CNN model to classify tweets into hate speech, offensive language, or neither. On a labeled Twitter dataset, the model achieved 91% accuracy, 91% precision, 90% recall, and 90% F1-score, although some hate tweets were misclassified. Njagi et al. [36] developed a lexicon-based hate speech detection method focusing on race, nationality, and religion. Their approach used subjectivity analysis to filter objective content and applied sentiment polarity and semantic features to build a hate classifier, highlighting challenges in capturing contextual nuance. Sharma et al. [37] proposed an ML and natural language processing (NLP)-based approach for detecting cyberbullying and aggressive comments in social media text. Their system analyzes user comments to identify harmful content and serves as a prototype for automated insult detection.

While early studies focused on English, recent research has expanded to other languages. Varade et al. [38] proposed a hate speech detection method for code-mixed Hinglish social media texts, using Word2Vec embeddings and LSTM to address the challenges of low-resource, multilingual data. Plaza-Del-Arco et al. [39] created Spanish language hate speech corpora targeting women and immigrants and demonstrated that monolingual models, such as BETO, outperform multilingual models in classification tasks. Albadi et al. [40] introduced the first Arabic dataset and lexicon for religious hate speech detection on Twitter. They compared lexicon-based, n-gram, and DL models and found that a GRU-based RNN with pre-trained embeddings achieved 0.84 AUROC, highlighting the challenges posed by Arabic's linguistic complexity. Raufi et al. [19] developed an Albanian corpus for mobile applications. Sreelakshmi et al. [41] developed a ML approach for detecting hate speech in Hindi-English code-mixed social media texts, using FastText embeddings and SVM-RBF classifiers. Their results show that FastText outperforms Word2Vec and doc2Vec, and that character-level features are particularly effective for code-mixed language processing. Alfina et al. [42] developed a new dataset for hate speech detection in Indonesian, covering religion, race, ethnicity, and gender-based hate. They conducted a preliminary study comparing various features and classifiers, with word n-grams and RF achieving the best F1 score of 93.5%. The study significantly contributes to non-English hate speech research.

To improve performance, ensemble models combining multiple classifiers were proposed. Paschalides et al. [43] introduced MANDOLA, a big-data system for detecting and monitoring online hate speech. The platform integrated multiple components for data collection, visualization, and classification, and included an ensemble-based algorithm shown to enhance detection performance. Araque et al. [44] proposed a sentiment-aware ensemble framework for hate speech and radicalization detection, combining affective features from AffectiveSpace and SenticNet with traditional representations like TF-IDF and SIMON. Experiments across five datasets showed improved performance and robustness. Waseem et al. [45] employed multi-task learning to transfer knowledge across hate speech domains, improving generalization. Del Vigna et al. [46] combined SVMs and LSTM models with sentiment lexicons and word embeddings for Facebook comment analysis.

Datasets play a crucial role in hate speech research. Waseem et al. [16] provided a 16,000-tweet dataset labeled for racism, sexism, or none, emphasizing annotation guidelines. Davidson et al. [17] created a 25,000-tweet dataset with three classes (hate, offensive, neutral). Lynn et al. [47] introduced a publicly available dataset of 2,285 Urban Dictionary entries annotated for misogyny by domain experts, supporting research in misogynistic language detection. de Gibert et al. [48] released a publicly available hate speech dataset derived from the white supremacist forum Stormfront, with manual annotations and baseline classification benchmarks. Ombui et al. [49] introduced a hate speech annotation framework based on Sternberg's theory, applied to 5,000 Kenyan election-related tweets to support supervised ML. Qian et al. [50] introduced a novel hate speech intervention task and released two benchmark datasets from Reddit and Gab, including contextual conversations, hate speech labels, and human-written responses. Wullach et al. [51] used a deep generative model to create a synthetic dataset of 1 million hate and non-hate sequences, demonstrating that augmenting training data improves model generalizability across hate speech benchmarks. Challenges such as dataset imbalance were addressed using techniques like SMOTE, as noted by Biere et al. [35].

Recent works have emphasized the importance of context. Basak et al. [52] proposed a taxonomy of public shaming types on Twitter, developed a classification system to detect them, analyzed shamer behavior, and introduced a mitigation tool (BlockShame) for real-time intervention. Chen et al. [53] proposed the lexical syntactic feature architecture for detecting offensive language and offensive users on social media, using a combination of lexical patterns, syntactic rules, and stylistic features. Dinakar et al. [54] applied common-sense reasoning via a bullying-specific knowledge base (BullySpace) to detect cyberbullying on social media, while also proposing empathetic user interface designs to aid intervention. Burnap et al. [55] incorporated user activity meta-information to improve Twitter hate speech detection accuracy. Pelzer et al. [56] analyzed directed hate speech with user-specific metadata. Lee et al. [57] proposed a personality-based DL approach, incorporating user traits to enhance classification.

Beyond Twitter, studies targeted other platforms. Del Vigna et al. [46] analyzed 17,567 Facebook comments for hate speech. Salminen et al. [31] developed a cross-platform classifier addressing platform-specific hate speech patterns. Hosseinmardi et al. [58] analyzed cyberbullying on Instagram, using multimodal text and image features. Rodriguez et al. [59] combined sentiment and emotion analysis for Facebook hate speech detection. Niam et al. [60] developed a system for detecting hate speech from images using text extracted from visuals. Using latent semantic analysis, they achieved moderate performance, showing initial steps toward image-based hate speech detection.

Many researchers focused on hate speech subtypes. Plaza-Del-Arco et al. [39] targeted misogyny and xenophobia in Spanish tweets. Miró-Llinares et al. [61] detected hate speech in Twitter digital microenvironments, emphasizing context-specific detection. Martins et al. [62] incorporated emotional analysis for hate speech detection, capturing the emotional context.

Despite all advancements, significant challenges remain in areas such as low-resource languages, domain adaptation, model explainability, and robustness against adversarial attacks. Gröndahl et al. [63] demonstrated how adversaries evade detection through subtle text modifications. Paetzold et al. [64] proposed a minimalistic RNN model for the HatEval shared task and achieved 7th place out of 62 in English Subtask A, demonstrating robustness in detecting hate speech in noisy Twitter data. Mossie et al. [65] identified vulnerable communities through hate speech detection, advocating for community-focused protection. Magu et al. [66] addressed implicit hate speech detection, tackling challenges related to coded language.

2.2 Turkish hateful analysis

Although significant strides have been made in analyzing hate speech in major world languages, the exploration of this phenomenon in Turkish remains limited. Early studies in Turkish primarily targeted general offensive language patterns, and only recently has the field seen methodological advances, such as the use of DL models and contextualized embeddings.

Involved in the analysis of user comments on Turkish news websites through manually labeled datasets and classical ML techniques for hate speech classification [5]. Another large-scale project collected 36,232 Turkish tweets over an 18-month period, identifying that approximately 19% of the corpus included offensive content. Tweets were classified not only by offensiveness but also by whether the content was targeted and the type of offense. ML models achieved F1 scores of 77.3% for offense identification, 77.9% for detecting targeted content, and 53.0% for classifying the offense type [5].

For social media platforms beyond Twitter, Karayiğit et al. [2] applied a hybrid approach combining CNN and classical ML to detect abusive language in Turkish Instagram comments. Their work underlined the effectiveness of DL in identifying abusive language in diverse data sources, extending applicability to less-studied platforms such as Instagram.

Another important dataset comprising 10,224 Turkish tweets was developed, labeled as "hate," "offensive," or "neutral." Hate-labeled tweets were further grouped into categories such as ethnic, religious, sexist, and political, with results indicating that 22.8% of all tweets were hate speech [6]. Comparative studies that tested both traditional ML models and DL architectures found BERT-based models to be the most successful, achieving 87.78% accuracy compared to 84.66% via SVM [7].

In the SemEval 2020 shared task OffensEval, Turkish was one of the participating languages. A multilingual model incorporating BERT and CNN achieved a macro-averaged F1 score of 0.814 for Turkish, ranking third overall [8]. Reflecting this multilingual trend, Karayiğit et al. [4] explored homophobic and hate speech detection using the multilingual-BERT model on Turkish social media data.

Their findings demonstrated that pre-trained multilingual models could effectively capture nuanced hate speech, especially in context-sensitive domains, even when trained on relatively low-resource languages like Turkish.

Further specialized datasets focused on controversial topics such as the Istanbul Convention and refugee rights. Using these topic-specific corpora, researchers applied BERTurk – a Transformer model tailored for the Turkish language – achieving classification accuracy rates of 77% and 71%, respectively [9].

The performance of ChatGPT was also tested on Turkish hate speech detection using a manually annotated corpus of 1,000 tweets. The model demonstrated competence comparable to fine-tuned BERT-based models, confirming its potential for use in low-resource NLP tasks [10]. Separately, a BERT-Base model trained on labeled social media data was deployed as a real-time content moderation system for Turkish, achieving a test accuracy of 92.53% in detecting harmful content [11].

Innovations like TurkishBERTweet – the first large-scale Turkish language model pre-trained on 900 million tweets – have further advanced the field. The model outperformed prior architectures across various tasks, including hate speech detection and sentiment classification [12]. Additional progress was achieved through the Turkish HatePrint corpus and the development of HateTargetBERT, a model that incorporates target-specific linguistic features within the Transformer architecture to boost performance and interpretability [13]. The adoption of DL, multilingual models, and domain-specific corpora signifies a shift toward more nuanced and robust solutions for identifying harmful content in Turkish digital discourse.

3. Materials and methods

This section presents the details of the dataset used for the experiments and a summary of the classification algorithms.

3.1 The Homophobic–Abusive Turkish Comments (HATC) dataset

The HATC dataset used in our study consists of Instagram comments obtained from accounts with potential homophobic content, as well as hate speech comments from the previously developed ATC (abusive turkish comments) dataset [4]. The HATC dataset includes comments containing sexist, homophobic, derogatory, and profane expressions, collected from Turkish magazine pages, football teams, and football players' Instagram accounts [4].

Homophobic comments were identified among the insult-labeled entries in the ATC dataset and were combined with additional homophobic comments gathered from Instagram. These were manually categorized as "homophobic," while sexist, derogatory, and profane expressions were labeled as "hate speech." The remaining comments were classified as "neutral." In total, the HATC dataset comprises 31,290 Instagram comments: 1,226 homophobic, 10,237 hate speech, and 19,827 neutral. The Instagram API and the Python programming language were used for data collection.

The labeling of comments in the HATC dataset was conducted by two researchers following the guidelines of the Big Slang Dictionary and the Turkish Language Association. The most frequently used homophobic expression was "top" ("ball"; homophobic slur targeting gay men), including diminutive/euphemistic variants such as "topitoş" (diminutive variant of the "top" slur) and "topitop" (candy brand name used euphemistically for the same slur). Other words categorized as homophobic included "puşt" (derogatory slur, often used homophobically), "ibne" (homophobic slur targeting gay men), and "lavuk" (derogatory slang roughly meaning "punk/jerk"; treated as homophobic in our corpus when used to target sexual orientation). Additionally, comments that conveyed homophobia through emojis without explicit text were labeled accordingly, while irrelevant emojis were removed from the dataset.

In Turkish social media discourse, certain emojis are contextually associated with homophobic expressions. During the data annotation process, emojis were labeled as homophobic when they implicitly conveyed discriminatory meaning related to sexual orientation, even when no explicit textual slur was present. Specifically, the ⚽ (U+26BD), 🏐 (U+1F3D0), and 👌 (U+1F44C) emojis were marked as homophobic because, in Turkish colloquial usage, these symbols are frequently used to imply that a person is homosexual – the first two representing the slang term "top" (a common homophobic slur) and the latter often accompanying such usage to intensify the mockery. Therefore, when these emojis appeared individually or jointly in comments, they were treated as homophobic content. The labeling was carried out automatically for these specific emojis within the dataset because the comments were collected from Instagram accounts that are known to contain homophobic material (e.g., @utandiran_paylasimlar, @kerimcandurmaz, @sametlicina). These accounts were identified as potential sources of homophobic discourse; therefore, all occurrences of the mentioned emojis within comments from these sources were automatically tagged as homophobic during the pre-processing stage. In contrast, other emojis unrelated to the homophobic context – such as 😂 (U+1F602) or 🌸 (U+1F338) – were regarded as irrelevant and removed from the dataset because they did not contribute semantic or contextual meaning associated with hate speech. This distinction ensured that the emoji-based annotations accurately reflected homophobic intent rather than general emotion or emphasis.

3.2 Methods

In this study, instead of traditional ML approaches, modern pre-trained Transformer-based language models were preferred for hate speech detection. The models used include ELECTRA-TR, XLM-RoBERTa (XLM-R), A Lite BERT for Turkish (ALBERT-TR), Robustly optimized BERT approach for Turkish (RoBERTa-TR), DistilBERT-TR, BERTurk, and Convolutional BERT for Turkish

(ConvBERTurk). These models demonstrate diversity in both their architectural structures and their capacity to be pre-trained on Turkish language data. Each model was fine-tuned on the HATC dataset and integrated into the training process. A total of seven different models were trained and evaluated using various performance metrics. A schematic representation of the methodology applied in this study is presented in **Figure 1**.

3.2.1 Data preparation and tokenization

In the initial phase of the study, the HATC dataset was loaded, and the columns named "message" and "label" were renamed to "text" and "labels," respectively, for compatibility with the standard input format required by the Hugging Face datasets library. Following this, the dataset was randomly split into training and testing subsets using an 80–20% ratio. This division was performed using stratified sampling based on the "labels" column to maintain the original class distribution across both subsets – an essential step, particularly due to the imbalanced nature of hate speech data.

For each Transformer model evaluated in this study, a dedicated AutoTokenizer was loaded. This tokenizer was responsible for converting raw input text into numerical representations by generating input_ids and attention_mask tensors compatible with the neural models. The tokenization process included breaking text into subword units, and to standardize input length, all sequences were either

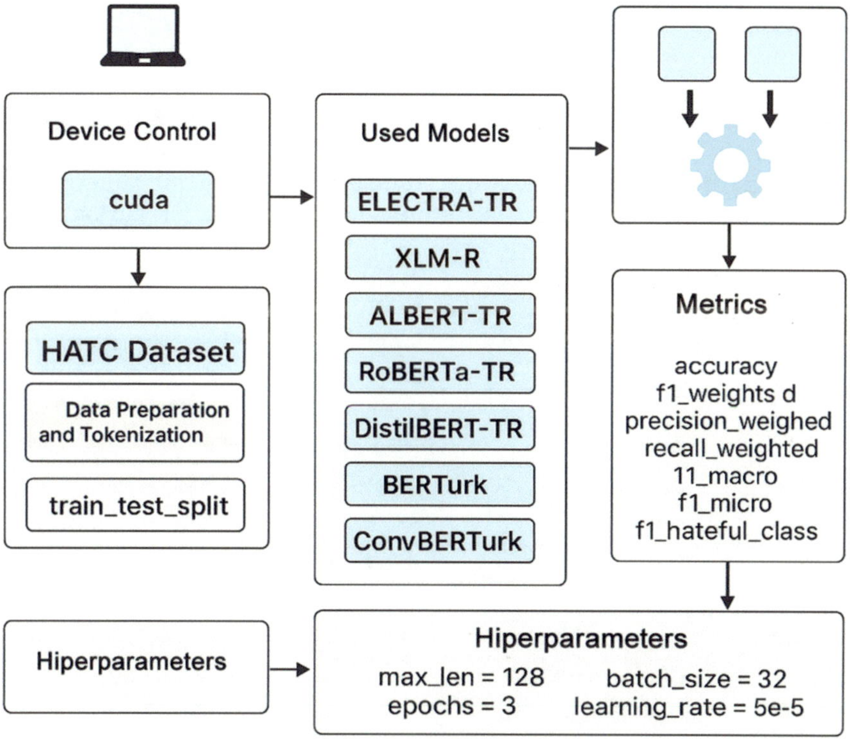

Figure 1.
Overview of the proposed hate speech detection methodology.

padded or truncated to a maximum length of 128 tokens. Finally, unnecessary columns were removed from the tokenized datasets, which were then converted into PyTorch tensor format to ensure efficient compatibility with the subsequent training pipeline.

3.2.2 Transformer-based models

This study conducted a comprehensive comparative analysis of seven advanced Transformer-based language models, specifically chosen for their superior capability in extracting and encoding contextual semantic information from Turkish text. Distinct from traditional ML models that necessitate explicit feature engineering, these models inherently learn rich, dense representations of linguistic nuances through their extensive pre-training on vast text corpora.

The models rigorously evaluated included ELECTRA-TR, a Turkish-specific ELECTRA discriminator model known for its strong performance in Turkish NLP tasks via token prediction; XLM-R, a highly effective multilingual model trained on an expansive dataset covering 100 languages, exhibiting robust cross-lingual transfer capabilities and exceptional performance for Turkish; ALBERT-TR, a parameter-efficient variant of BERT optimized for reduced memory footprint and faster inference without significant performance degradation, specifically pre-trained on Turkish data; RoBERTa-TR, an optimized BERT pre-training approach tailored for Turkish; DistilBERT-TR, utilizing a compressed BERT architecture; BERTurk, based on the original BERT architecture; and ConvBERTurk, employing a convolutional BERT architecture. All models were fine-tuned on the HATC dataset using AutoModelForSequenceClassification for sequence classification. The details of the evaluated models, including architecture, pre-trained checkpoints, and parameter sizes, are summarized in **Table 1**.

ELECTRA aims to increase efficiency in the training process by adopting the RTD approach instead of masked language modeling. The ELECTRA-TR model (dbmdz/electra-base-turkish-cased-discriminator) is a version trained in the Turkish language, producing representations more suitable for Turkish language features. In this study, classification was performed using AutoModelForSequenceClassification with the contextual vector obtained from the (CLS) token as the classification layer. XLM-R is a multilingual variant of RoBERTa trained on data from over 100 languages. It delivers strong performance

Model	Architecture	Pre-trained checkpoint	Parameters
ELECTRA-TR	Discriminator	dbmdz/electra-base-turkish-cased	110 M
XLM-R	RoBERTa-based	xlm-roberta-base	270 M
ALBERT-TR	Lite BERT	dbmdz/albert-base-turkish	12 M
RoBERTa-TR	Optimized BERT	TURKCELL/roberta-base-turkish	125 M
DistilBERT-TR	Compressed BERT	dbmdz/distilbert-base-turkish	66 M
BERTurk	Original BERT	dbmdz/bert-base-turkish	110 M
ConvBERTurk	Convolutional BERT	dbmdz/convbert-base-turkish	110 M

Table 1.
Overview of the seven Transformer-based models fine-tuned for Turkish hateful analysis.

across both high-resource and low-resource languages. For classification, the model leverages sentence-level representations derived from the (CLS) token. Due to its multilingual architecture, XLM-R is capable of effectively capturing contextual semantic relationships in Turkish texts.

ALBERT is a parameter-efficient version of the BERT architecture designed to reduce training time through extensive parameter sharing. ALBERT-TR (dbmdz/albert-base-turkish) is a Turkish-optimized version with only 12 million parameters, yet it maintains high performance in various NLP tasks despite its compact size. RoBERTa, an enhanced variant of BERT, improves performance through more robust pre-training techniques. RoBERTa-TR (TURKCELL/roberta-base-turkish-uncased) is trained exclusively on Turkish texts, enabling it to more effectively model Turkish language contexts. With 125 million parameters, the model has demonstrated strong results in Turkish text classification tasks.

DistilBERT-TR (dbmdz/distilbert-base-turkish-cased) is a distilled version of BERT, designed to retain most of BERT's language understanding capabilities while operating with a significantly smaller model size (66 M parameters). It offers a favorable trade-off between speed and accuracy. BERTurk (dbmdz/bert-base-turkish-cased) is a Turkish-specific implementation of the original BERT architecture. With 110 million parameters, it is fine-tuned for Turkish language understanding and shows robust performance across a range of Turkish NLP tasks. ConvBERTurk (dbmdz/convbert-base-turkish-cased) extends the BERT architecture by incorporating convolutional layers to better capture local dependencies. Also containing 110 million parameters, this architecture enhances the model's ability to learn fine-grained patterns in Turkish text.

3.2.3 Training methodology

Each selected Transformer model underwent a fine-tuning process on the HATC dataset, specifically targeting hate speech classification. The entire training workflow was orchestrated using Hugging Face's Trainer API, which efficiently managed training loops, performance evaluation, and metric computations. Training was conducted on a graphics processing unit (GPU) when available, otherwise falling back to central processing unit acceleration. Key hyperparameters were carefully standardized to ensure consistency across all models. Each model was trained for three epochs with a fixed batch size of 32 for both training and evaluation. The Adam optimizer was used for gradient-based optimization, with weight decay set to 0.01 as a form of L2 regularization to mitigate overfitting. A constant learning rate scheduler was applied without any warm-up steps.

Model performance was evaluated at the end of each epoch using a held-out test set. Evaluation metrics were computed via a custom "compute_metrics" function, reporting accuracy, weighted F1-score, macro F1, micro F1, and, importantly, "f1_hateful_class," which reflects the F1-score of the positive (hateful) class. To improve runtime performance, external logging services such as Weights and Biases were disabled via "report_to" = "none," and internal logging mechanisms were used instead. After each model's training and evaluation cycle, GPU memory was explicitly released using "torch.cuda.empty_cache()" and "gc.collect()." This memory management strategy helped prevent hardware bottlenecks and ensured consistent performance across model comparisons.

3.2.4 Performance metrics

To comprehensively evaluate the performance of the fine-tuned Transformer models in hate speech detection, a set of standard classification metrics was employed. These metrics are particularly important for tasks involving imbalanced datasets, such as hate speech classification, where accuracy alone may provide a misleading picture of model performance. The evaluation metrics included:

- Accuracy, which measures the proportion of correctly predicted instances out of the total number of samples,;
- Precision, defined as the ratio of true positive predictions to the total number of predicted positives, reflects the quality of positive predictions.
- Recall (sensitivity), which captures the model's ability to identify all actual positive instances, is calculated as the ratio of true positives (TPs) to the total actual positives.
- F1-Score, the harmonic mean of Precision and Recall, offers a balanced metric especially suitable for imbalanced class distributions.

For holistic performance analysis in the binary classification setting, weighted averaging was applied to Precision, Recall, and F1-Score. In this approach, metrics are computed for each class and then averaged according to the number of true instances per class, thereby reflecting the class distribution in the overall score.

Importantly, the f1_hateful_class metric – representing the F1 score for the positive (hate speech) class – was designated as the primary criterion for identifying the best-performing model, given the critical importance of accurately detecting hate-related content. The evaluation process involved generating predictions on the test set for each model, computing the above-mentioned metrics, and compiling the results into a comparative table for further analysis.

4. Experimental setup and results

All experiments for this study were carried out in the Google Colaboratory environment, harnessing its GPU acceleration capabilities. This cloud-based Jupyter Notebook environment provided a setup-free platform for our DL tasks. The entire framework was developed in Python 3, relying on a specialized suite of libraries designed for efficient Transformer model processing and training. To streamline execution and avoid external logging, integration with Weights and Biases was explicitly disabled. Training and evaluation loops efficiently utilized available GPU resources, and after each model's cycle, the GPU cache was cleared to optimize hardware utilization for subsequent processes. Our experiments focused on binary hate speech classification (neutral vs. hate) using the HATC dataset. We applied a stratified 80/20 train-test split to ensure consistent class distribution between the training and testing subsets. Each of the seven Transformer-based DL models was fine-tuned for 3 epochs, using a batch size of 32, a learning rate of 5e-5, and an Adam optimizer with a weight decay of 0.01. Performance was thoroughly evaluated using metrics like accuracy, weighted precision, weighted recall, weighted F1-score, macro F1-score, micro F1-score, and, critically, the F1-score for the hateful class.

Training time refers to how long it took to fine-tune each model on the 80% training subset, while testing time indicates the duration required to evaluate the fine-tuned model on the 20% test subset. The detailed experimental results for each of the seven distinct Transformer models in this hate speech detection study will be presented in the subsequent subsections, showcasing their performance across these defined metrics.

4.1 Experimental results of Transformer-based models

The performance of the seven fine-tuned Transformer-based models on the HATC dataset for binary hate speech classification is summarized in **Table 2**. The models, evaluated on metrics such as accuracy, weighted precision, weighted recall, weighted F1-score, macro F1-score, micro F1-score, and, critically, the F1-score for the hateful class, demonstrate strong capabilities in detecting hate speech within Turkish social media comments.

As **Table 1** illustrates, the ELECTRA-TR model (dbmdz/electra-base-turkish-cased-discriminator) emerged as the top performer. It achieved the highest F1-score for the hateful class at 0.9507. This finding is particularly significant, given the imbalanced nature of hate speech datasets and the critical importance of accurately identifying positive (hateful) instances. ELECTRA-TR also demonstrated leading performance across other key metrics, including accuracy (0.9661), weighted F1-score (0.9661), and macro F1-score (0.9633), aligning with the claims made in the abstract.

Following ELECTRA-TR, the ConvBERTurk model showed strong performance, with an F1-score for the hateful class of 0.9498 and consistently high overall metrics. BERTurk also presented commendable results, achieving an F1-score of 0.9472 for the hateful class. These results highlight the effectiveness of language-specific Transformer models pre-trained on Turkish data. They generally outperformed the multilingual XLM-R model, which had an F1-score of 0.9429 for the hateful class, in capturing the intricate morphological and semantic nuances of Turkish hate speech.

The ALBERT-TR model, despite its significantly lower parameter count (12 M) compared to other models, still achieved a respectable F1-score of 0.9327 for the hateful class, demonstrating its parameter efficiency. Both RoBERTa-TR and DistilBERT-TR also delivered robust performance, with hateful class F1-scores of 0.9392 and 0.9366, respectively.

These findings strongly suggest that while multilingual models like XLM-R can achieve solid results, models explicitly pre-trained for Turkish, such as ELECTRA-TR, ConvBERTurk, and BERTurk, are better suited for the complexities of Turkish hate speech detection due to their specialized understanding of the language. The superior performance of ELECTRA-TR specifically validates its RTD pre-training objective as highly effective for downstream classification tasks.

A close examination of each model's matrix reveals specific strengths and weaknesses in its classification capabilities, as illustrated in **Figure 2**. ELECTRA-TR emerges as a standout performer, exhibiting the highest number of true positives (TPs), reaching an impressive 2,135, coupled with the lowest number of False Negatives (FNs) at 158. This combination unequivocally demonstrates its superior ability to accurately identify hateful comments. Furthermore, its relatively low count

Model	Accuracy	Precision_weighted	Recall_weighted	F1_weighted	F1_micro	F1_macro	f1_hateful_class
ELECTRA-TR	0.9661	0.9661	0.9661	0.9661	0.9661	0.9633	0.9507
XLM-R	0.9591	0.9592	0.9591	0.9591	0.9591	0.9555	0.9429
ALBERT-TR	0.9490	0.9490	0.9490	0.9490	0.9490	0.9446	0.9327
RoBERTa-TR	0.9556	0.9555	0.9556	0.9556	0.9556	0.9520	0.9392
DistilBERT-TR	0.9537	0.9536	0.9537	0.9537	0.9537	0.9499	0.9366
BERTurk	0.9626	0.9627	0.9626	0.9626	0.9626	0.9594	0.9472
ConvBERTurk	0.9652	0.9652	0.9652	0.9652	0.9652	0.9623	0.9498

Table 2.
Experimental results of Transformer-based models on the HATC dataset.

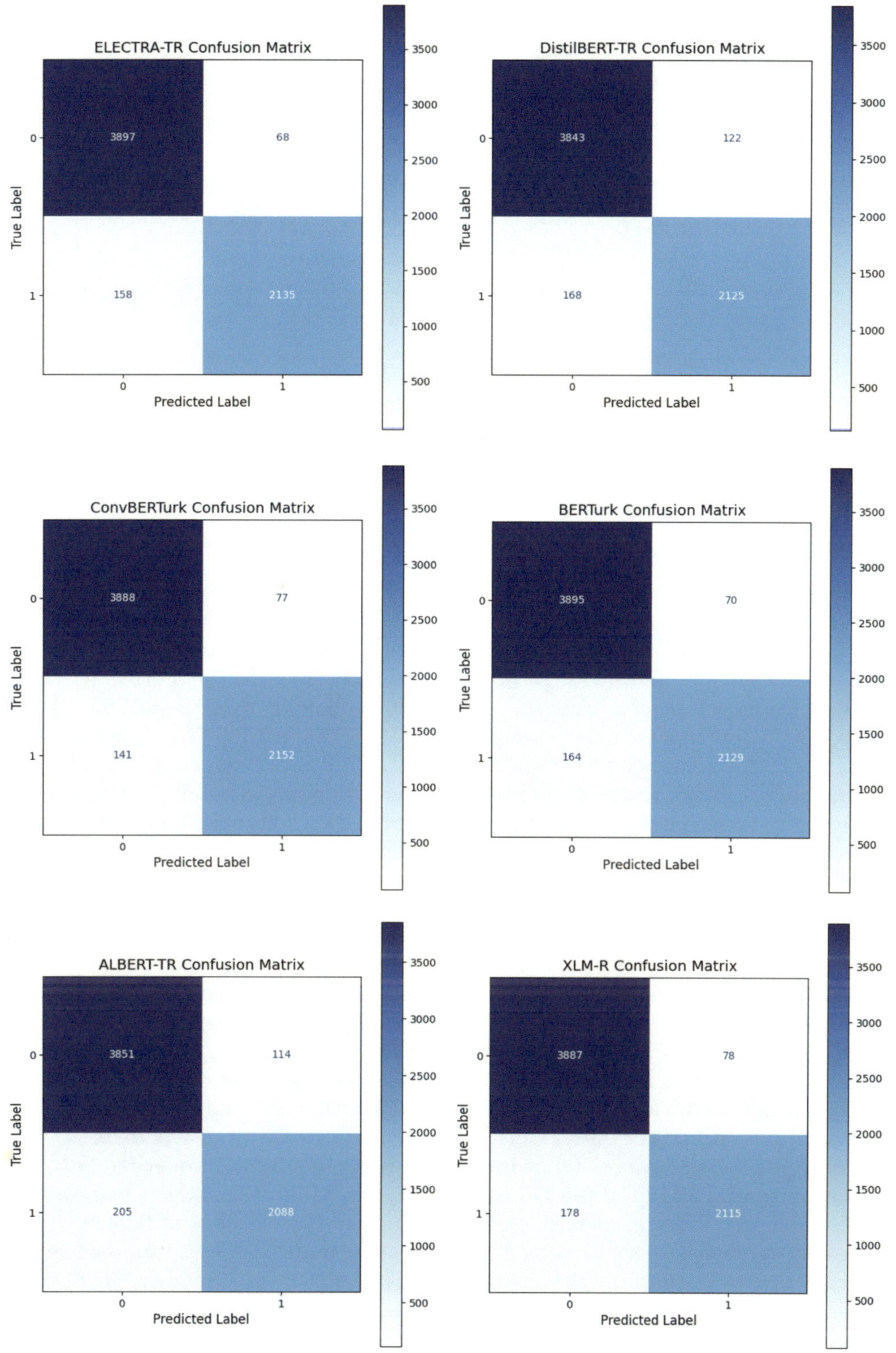

Figure 2.
Confusion matrices of Transformer-based models on the HATC dataset.

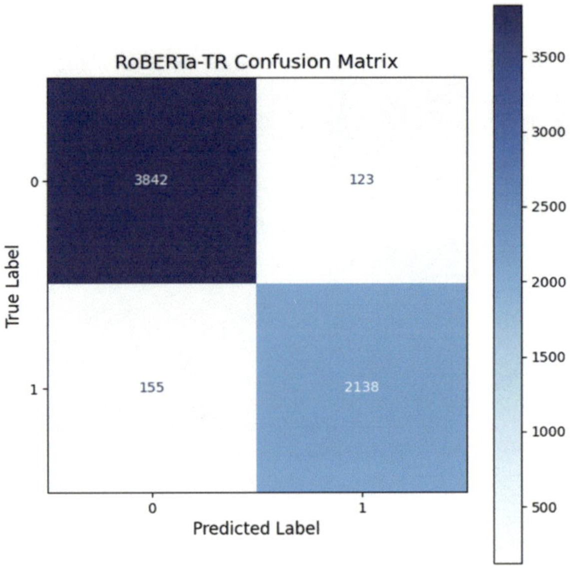

Figure 2.
Continue.

of False Positives (FPs), at just 68, underscores its precision. This robust performance in pinpointing the positive class (hateful speech) is in perfect harmony with its leading f1_hateful_class score of 0.9507. Following this, DistilBERT-TR presents a commendable balance, registering 2,125 TPs and 168 FN. However, its FPs, at 122, are notably higher than those of ELECTRA-TR, suggesting a slightly increased propensity to misclassify non-hateful comments as hateful, a tendency reflected in its f1_hateful_class of 0.9366. ConvBERTurk also delivers a remarkably strong performance, with 2,152 TPs and 141 FNs, marking it as highly effective in detecting hate speech. Its FPs, at 77, are also maintained at a very low level, providing visual evidence that strongly supports its high f1_hateful_class of 0.9498, a score strikingly close to ELECTRA-TR's. BERTurk further reinforces the trend of strong performance with 2,129 TPs and 164 FNs, and impressively boasts one of the lowest FPs at 70, indicating excellent specificity; this performance aligns seamlessly with its f1_hateful_class of 0.9472. Moving to ALBERT-TR, while its performance remains reasonably acceptable, it shows a lower count of TPs (2088) and a higher number of FNs (205) when compared to the top-tier models. Its FPs, at 114, are also higher than those of ELECTRA-TR, ConvBERTurk, and BERTurk, reflecting its comparatively lower f1_hateful_class of 0.9327, a characteristic the article attributes to its significantly reduced parameter count. The multilingual XLM-R model demonstrates competence with 2,115 TPs and 178 FNs, and its FPs, at 78, are relatively low. Despite its capable performance, its metrics, including an f1_hateful_class of 0.9429, are generally surpassed by the leading Turkish-specific models, thereby supporting the article's assertion regarding the advantage of language-specific models. Finally, RoBERTa-TR achieves 2,138 TPs with 155 FNs, indicating a good recall for the hateful class. However, its FPs, at 173, are notably higher than most other models, suggesting a greater inclination toward false alarms. Its f1_hateful_class stands at 0.9392. In conclusion, the visual data presented in these confusion matrices unequivocally confirms that ELECTRA-TR consistently exhibits the most optimal balance between accurately identifying positive instances (TPs) and minimizing misclassifications (FNs and FPs), showing particular excellence in the detection of hateful comments. Furthermore, ConvBERTurk and BERTurk also demonstrate exceptionally strong performance. The elevated FNs observed for ALBERT-TR suggest a greater tendency to miss hateful comments, whereas the higher FPs for RoBERTa-TR and DistilBERT-TR indicate an increased rate of incorrectly flagging non-hateful comments as hateful. The confusion matrices results for the models in **Figure 2** are largely in agreement with the quantitative results presented in **Table 2**, collectively supporting the general conclusion that Turkish-specific models, with ELECTRA-TR at the forefront, are remarkably effective for the complex task of Turkish hate speech detection.

In culmination, the comprehensive analysis of these confusion matrices visually confirms that the ELECTRA-TR model consistently achieves the optimal balance between accurately identifying positive instances (TPs) and minimizing misclassifications (both FNs and FPs), thereby demonstrating exceptional proficiency in the detection of hateful comments. ConvBERTurk and BERTurk also exhibit very strong performance characteristics. Conversely, the elevated FNs observed for ALBERT-TR imply a tendency to miss a greater proportion of hateful comments, while the higher FPs for RoBERTa-TR and DistilBERT-TR indicate more frequent incorrect flagging of non-hateful comments as hateful.

4.2 Performance and error analysis

The ELECTRA-TR model, which achieved the highest performance with an accuracy of 96.61% and an F1-macro score of 96.33% on the test set of the HATC dataset, accurately classified 6,032 out of 6,258 test instances. However, a total of 226 instances were misclassified, comprising 158 false negatives (FNs) and 68 false positives (FPs). This section systematically analyzes these errors to identify their underlying causes and patterns, focusing on the types of expressions that particularly challenged the model, supported by representative examples from ELECTRA-TR's mispredictions.

FN denote instances where the model failed to identify hate speech or homophobic comments, instead classifying them as non-hateful. A considerable portion of these errors involved indirect or context-dependent expressions, where the model struggled to detect the implicit hateful intent. For instance, the comment "bu şimdi neye benzemiş 🤭 💩 💩#paramvarzevkimyok" ("what does this even look like 🤭 💩 💩#Ihavemoneybutnotaste," a sarcastic insult implying mockery and disgust) was misclassified as non-hateful despite its clear derogatory and hateful content. Similarly, the expression "Evli ve çocuğu olduğu halde başkasıyla gezen kadın ekranlarda normal hayatına devam ediyor. suç bizde" ("Even though she is married and has a child, she goes on with another man on TV – the shame is on us," a judgmental and accusatory statement), which contains strong accusatory and potentially hateful language, was also incorrectly predicted as non-hateful. These cases collectively underscore the model's inherent difficulty in detecting indirect or contextually complex hate speech.

FPs occurred when non-hateful comments were incorrectly classified as hate speech. These errors were often triggered by emotionally charged or critically worded language that the model misinterpreted. For example, the comment "Kokoş lar toplanmış 🤣🤣" ("The flashy ones have gathered 🤣🤣," a lighthearted, possibly ironic remark) was falsely classified as hate speech, despite appearing to be a casual or ironic statement without explicit hateful intent. Similarly, "olum biz bu gülüşü trollüğüne yapıyoruz adamlar para veriyor" (Bro, we do this laugh just for trolling, and they actually pay for it), though critical in tone, appears to reference social media trends rather than targeted aggression. These examples suggest that the model may sometimes over-rely on emotionally charged keywords or certain emojis without fully capturing the broader pragmatic context or the subtle nuances of Turkish internet slang.

The confusion matrix for ELECTRA-TR, visually represented, offers a clear depiction of the distribution of correct and incorrect predictions for this binary classification task. It accurately classified 3,897 non-hateful comments (TNs) and 2,135 hateful comments (TPs). Conversely, it misclassified 68 non-hateful comments as hateful (FPs) and 158 hateful comments as non-hateful (FNs). These specific patterns unequivocally confirm the model's strength in detecting explicit hate speech but simultaneously highlight persistent challenges in effectively handling implicit and context-dependent expressions.

To systematically address these identified error patterns, future research should prioritize augmenting the training dataset with a more diverse range of examples encompassing indirect, sarcastic, and contextually nuanced hate speech. Incorporating contextual embeddings that can capture broader discourse or user interaction patterns could significantly enhance the model's ability to detect implicit hateful content. Additionally, exploring advanced techniques such as adversarial training or fine-tuning on datasets specifically curated for sarcasm detection may further improve the model's sensitivity to non-literal expressions. These findings collectively underscore ELECTRA-TR's inherent robustness for explicit hate speech detection while concurrently pinpointing critical areas for improvement in navigating the complex linguistic and contextual intricacies of the Turkish language within social media environments.

5. Discussion

The ELECTRA-TR model developed in this study achieved state-of-the-art performance on the HATC dataset, with F1-macro and F1-micro scores of 96%, surpassing previous benchmarks in Turkish hate speech detection. To contextualize these results, we compare our model's performance with existing studies in Turkish NLP, as shown in **Table 3**.

As illustrated in **Table 3**, prior studies primarily focused on general hate speech or offensive language, often using Twitter data, and achieved F1 scores ranging from 0.71 to 0.89. Karayiğit et al. (2021) employed a hybrid CNN-ML approach for homophobic and hate speech content detection on Instagram, achieving an F1-score of 0.89. While their work demonstrated the effectiveness of DL for platform-specific hate speech detection, our ELECTRA-TR model significantly outperforms these results, achieving a 7% improvement in F1-score. This advancement highlights the superiority of Transformer-based architectures, particularly those pre-trained on Turkish data, in capturing the morphological and contextual complexities of hate speech.

Study	Platform	Model	Dataset type	F1 score	Accuracy
[Çöltekin, 2020]	Twitter	SVM	General offensive tweets	0.773	0.779
[Safaya et al., 2020]	Twitter	Multilingual BERT + CNN	OffensEval Turkish	0.814	–
[Beyhan et al., 2022]	Twitter	BERTurk	Istanbul Convention tweets	0.71–0.77	0.71–0.77
[Bayrak et al., 2023]	Social Media	BERTurk (real-time)	General hate speech	–	0.925
[Karayiğit et al., 2021]	Instagram	CNN + ML Hybrid	HATC dataset	0.89	0.91
This study	Instagram	ELECTRA-TR	HATC (homophobic/abusive)	0.96	0.96

Table 3.
Comparison of our model with previous Turkish hate speech detection studies.

The superior performance of ELECTRA-TR can be attributed to its pre-training on Turkish-specific data and its RTD objective, which enhances its ability to capture nuanced expressions of hate, including homophobic slurs and implicit abuse. This aligns with findings from other languages, where language-specific Transformer models (e.g., BETO for Spanish, BERTurk for Turkish) have demonstrated significant advantages over multilingual counterparts (Plaza-Del-Arco et al. [39]). However, our error analysis revealed that the model occasionally struggles with indirect or sarcastic hate speech, a limitation also observed in related works (Mozafari et al. [24]; Behzadi et al. [26]). Future research could explore integrating contextual or user-level features, as well as adversarial training, to improve detection of implicit hate speech.

Another key contribution of this study lies in demonstrating significant performance improvements on the existing HATC dataset introduced by Karayiğit et al. [4]. While both studies focus on hate speech detection in homophobic and abusive Instagram comments, this work employs a more advanced Transformer-based model, ELECTRA-TR, achieving superior results (F1: 0.96) compared to the earlier CNN + ML hybrid approach (F1: 0.91). This highlights the effectiveness of language-specific Transformer models in capturing platform-specific linguistic patterns more accurately.

These contributions lay a strong foundation for future research, particularly in addressing implicit hate speech and expanding to other low-resource languages through transfer learning.

6. Conclusions

The automatic detection of hate speech, particularly homophobic and abusive content in Turkish social media, presents significant challenges due to the language's morphological complexity and the contextual nuances of online communication. This study addresses these challenges by introducing the HATC dataset – a comprehensive collection of manually annotated Instagram comments – and proposing an ELECTRA-based DL model specifically fine-tuned for Turkish. Our ELECTRA-TR model achieves remarkable performance, with F1-macro and F1-micro scores of 96%, surpassing existing benchmarks in Turkish hate speech detection.

A total of seven Transformer-based models were evaluated, including ELECTRA-TR, XLM-R, ALBERT-TR, RoBERTa-TR, DistilBERT-TR, BERTurk, and ConvBERTurk. Among these, ELECTRA-TR demonstrated superior performance, leveraging its RTD objective to effectively capture the morphological richness and contextual subtleties of Turkish hate speech. The model's ability to classify homophobic and abusive content with high precision and recall highlights its potential for real-world applications in content moderation. While multilingual models like XLM-R showed competitive results, language-specific models consistently outperformed them, reinforcing the importance of language-tailored architectures in NLP tasks.

This study makes significant contributions from methodological, practical, and academic perspectives. Methodologically, it represents the application of ELECTRA for Turkish hate speech detection, setting a new standard for performance in this domain. Practically, the proposed model can be deployed on social media platforms to automatically identify and filter harmful content, fostering safer online environments and protecting vulnerable communities.

However, certain limitations must be acknowledged. The HATC dataset is derived exclusively from Instagram, which may not fully represent hate speech dynamics on other platforms. Additionally, the model occasionally struggles with indirect or sarcastic expressions, a common challenge in hate speech detection. Future work could address these limitations by expanding the dataset to include multimodal content (e.g., text and images) and exploring advanced techniques such as adversarial training or context-aware embeddings to improve the detection of implicit hate speech. Further research could also investigate the integration of user behavior data or cross-lingual transfer learning to enhance model robustness.

In conclusion, this study establishes a strong foundation for hate speech detection in Turkish social media by introducing a high-performance ELECTRA-TR model. The model's exceptional accuracy and the dataset's richness offer valuable tools for researchers and practitioners aiming to combat online abuse. By bridging the gap between linguistic complexity and computational efficiency, this work paves the way for future advancements in Turkish NLP and content moderation systems. It also underscores the critical role of language-specific models in addressing the unique challenges of hate speech detection in morphologically rich languages like Turkish.

This study marks a significant step forward in the fight against online hate speech, providing both a technological solution and a scholarly resource to support safer digital spaces for Turkish-speaking communities.

Data availability

The primary dataset used in the current study is publicly available on the Kaggle platform. The HATC dataset, which contains 31,290 Turkish Instagram comments categorized as homophobic, hate speech, and neutral for detecting homophobic and hate speech content, can be obtained from https://www.kaggle.com/habibekarayiit/datasets.

Acknowledgment

The authors acknowledge the use of LLM for language polishing of the manuscript.

Author details

Habibe Karayiğit[1]* and Ali Akdagli[2]

1 General Directorate of Secondary Education, Ministry of National Education, Adana, Turkey

2 Department of Electrical and Electronics Engineering, Mersin University, Mersin, Turkey

*Address all correspondence to: habibekarayigit@aof.anadolu.edu.tr

IntechOpen

© 2025 The Author(s). Licensee IntechOpen. This chapter is distributed under the terms of the Creative Commons Attribution License (http://creativecommons.org/licenses/by/4.0/), which permits unrestricted use, distribution, and reproduction in any medium, provided the original work is properly cited. (cc) BY

References

[1] Durrant P. Formulaicity in an agglutinating language: The case of Turkish. Corpus Linguistics and Linguistic Theory. 2013;**9**(1):1–38. DOI: 10.1515/CLLT-2013-0009/MACHINEREADABLECITATION/RIS

[2] Karayiğit H, Acı Çİ, Akdağlı A. Detecting abusive Instagram comments in Turkish using convolutional neural network and machine learning methods. Expert Systems with Applications. 2021;**174**:114802. DOI: 10.1016/J.ESWA.2021.114802

[3] Bayram MA, *et al.*, "Setting standards in Turkish NLP: TR-MMLU for large language model evaluation," 2024. [Online]. Available from: https://arxiv.org/pdf/2501.00593 [Accessed: 2025-June-24]

[4] Karayiğit H, Akdagli A, Aci Çİ. Homophobic and hate speech detection using multilingual-BERT model on Turkish social media. Information Technology and Control. 2022;**51**(2):356–375. DOI: 10.5755/J01.ITC.51.2.29988

[5] Çöltekin Ç, "A corpus of Turkish offensive language on social media," 2020. [Online]. Available from: https://aclanthology.org/2020.lrec-1.758 [Accessed: 2024-August-29]

[6] Mayda I, Demir YE, Dalyan T, Diri B, "Hate speech dataset from Turkish tweets," *Proc. - 2021 Innov. Intell. Syst. Appl. Conf. ASYU 2021*, 2021, DOI: 10.1109/ASYU52992.2021.9599042

[7] Raj C, Agarwal A, Bharathy G, Narayan B, Prasad M. Cyberbullying detection: Hybrid models based on machine learning and natural language processing techniques. Electronics. 2021;**10**(22):2810. DOI: 10.3390/ELECTRONICS10222810

[8] Safaya A, Abdullatif M, Yuret D, "KUISAIL at SemEval-2020 task 12: BERT-CNN for offensive speech identification in social media," *14th Int. Work. Semant. Eval. SemEval 2020 - co-located 28th Int. Conf. Comput. Linguist. COLING 2020, Proc.*, pp. 2054–2059, Jul. 2020, DOI: 10.18653/v1/2020.semeval-1.271

[9] Beyhan F, *et al.*, "A Turkish hate speech dataset and detection system," 2022. [Online]. Available from: https://aclanthology.org/2022.lrec-1.443 [Accessed: 2024-August-29]

[10] Cam NB, Ozgur A, "Evaluation of ChatGPT and BERT-based models for Turkish hate speech detection," *UBMK 2023 - Proc. 8th Int. Conf. Comput. Sci. Eng.*, pp. 229–233, 2023, DOI: 10.1109/UBMK59864.2023.10286663

[11] Bayrak Ş, Karaca A, Toson F, Kocabey A, Arslanoglu FB, "Detection of hate speech in Turkish social media posts with BERT-base model," *31st IEEE Conf. Signal Process. Commun. Appl. SIU 2023*, 2023, DOI: 10.1109/SIU59756.2023.10224040

[12] Najafi A, Varol O. TurkishBERTweet: Fast and reliable large language model for social media analysis. Expert Systems with Applications. 2024;**255**:124737. DOI: 10.1016/J.ESWA.2024.124737

[13] Uludo˘ Gan G, *et al.*, "Detecting hate speech in Turkish print media: A corpus and a hybrid approach with target-oriented linguistic knowledge,"

2024. [Online]. Available from: https://aclanthology.org/2024.case-1.29 [Accessed: 2024-August-29]

[14] Greevy E, Smeaton AF, "Classifying racist texts using a support vector machine," *Proc. Sheff. SIGIR - Twenty-Seventh Annu. Int. ACM SIGIR Conf. Res. Dev. Inf. Retr.*, pp. 468–469, 2004, DOI: 10.1145/1008992.1009074; PAGE:STRING:ARTICLE/CHAPTER

[15] Warner W, Hirschberg J, "Detecting hate speech on the World Wide Web," Proc. Second Work. Lang. Soc. Media, pp. 19–26, 2012, [Online]. Available from: https://aclanthology.org/W12-2103 [Accessed: 2021-August-08]

[16] Waseem D, Zeerak, Hovy, "Hateful symbols or hateful people? Predictive features for hate speech detection on Twitter | Request PDF," in *Proceedings of the NAACL Student Research Workshop*, 2016, pp. 88–93. DOI: 10.18653/v1/N16-2013

[17] Davidson T, Warmsley D, Macy M, Weber I, "Automated hate speech detection and the problem of offensive language," in *Proceedings of the 11th Conference on Web and Social Media*, 2017. [Online]. Available from: http://arxiv.org/abs/1703.04009

[18] Sahi H, Kilic Y, Saglam RB. Automated detection of hate speech towards woman on Twitter. UBMK 2018 - 3rd International Conference on Computer Science and Engineering. 2018;533–536. DOI: 10.1109/UBMK.2018.8566304

[19] Raufi B, Xhaferri I, "Application of machine learning techniques for hate speech detection in mobile applications," *2018 Int. Conf. Inf. Technol. InfoTech 2018 - Proc.*, Oct. 2018, DOI: 10.1109/INFOTECH.2018.8510738

[20] Fatahillah NR, Suryati P, Haryawan C, "Implementation of Naive Bayes classifier algorithm on social media (Twitter) to the teaching of Indonesian hate speech," *Proc. - 2017 Int. Conf. Sustain. Inf. Eng. Technol. SIET 2017*, vol. **2018**, pp. 128–131, Jul. 2017, DOI: 10.1109/SIET.2017.8304122

[21] Badjatiya P, Gupta S, Gupta M, Varma V, "Deep learning for hate speech detection in tweets," *26th Int. World Wide Web Conf. 2017, WWW 2017 Companion*, pp. 759–760. 2017, DOI: 10.1145/3041021.3054223

[22] Gambäck B, Sikdar UK "(PDF) Using convolutional neural networks to classify hate-speech," in *Proceedings of the First Workshop on Abusive Language Online*, 2017, pp. 85–90. DOI: 10.18653/v1/W17-3013

[23] Pitsilis GK, Ramampiaro H, Langseth H. Effective hate-speech detection in Twitter data using recurrent neural networks. Applied Intelligence. 2018;**48**(12):4730–4742. DOI: 10.1007/S10489-018-1242-Y/METRICS

[24] Mozafari M, Farahbakhsh R, Crespi N. A BERT-based transfer learning approach for hate speech detection in online social media. Studies in Computational Intelligence. 2020;**881**:928–940. DOI: 10.1007/978-3-030-36687-2_77

[25] Mutanga TM, Mutanga RT, Naicker N, Olugbara OO. Hate speech detection in Twitter using transformer methods. Hate Speech Detection on Twitter Using Transformer Methods Article in International Journal of Advanced Computer Science and Applications. 2020;**11**(9). DOI: 10.14569/IJACSA.2020.0110972

[26] Behzadi M, Harris IG, Derakhshan A, “Rapid cyber-bullying detection method using compact BERT models,” *Proc. - 2021 IEEE 15th Int. Conf. Semant. Comput. ICSC 2021*, pp. 199–202, Jan. 2021, DOI: 10.1109/ICSC50631.2021.00042

[27] Sutejo TL, Lestari DP, “Indonesia hate speech detection using deep learning,” *Proc. 2018 Int. Conf. Asian Lang. Process. IALP 2018*, pp. 39–43, Jul. 2018, DOI: 10.1109/IALP.2018.8629154

[28] Saksesi AS, Nasrun M, Setianingsih C, “Analysis text of hate speech detection using recurrent neural network,” *Proc. - 2018 Int. Conf. Control. Electron. Renew. Energy Commun. ICCEREC 2018*, pp. 242–248, Jul. 2018, DOI: 10.1109/ICCEREC.2018.8712104

[29] Sazany E, Budi I, “Deep learning-based implementation of hate speech identification on texts in Indonesian: Preliminary study,” *Proc. ICAITI 2018 - 1st Int. Conf. Appl. Inf. Technol. Innov. Towar. A New Paradig. Des. Assist. Technol. Smart Home Care*, pp. 114–117, Jul. 2018, DOI: 10.1109/ICAITI.2018.8686725

[30] Setyadi NA, Nasrun M, Setianingsih C, “Text analysis for hate speech detection using backpropagation neural network,” *Proc. - 2018 Int. Conf. Control. Electron. Renew. Energy Commun. ICCEREC 2018*, pp. 159–165, Jul. 2018, DOI: 10.1109/ICCEREC.2018.8712109

[31] Salminen J, Hopf M, Chowdhury SA, Gyo Jung S, Almerekhi H, Jansen BJ. Developing an online hate classifier for multiple social media platforms. Human-centric Computing and Information Sciences. 2020;**10**(1):1–34. DOI: 10.1186/S13673-019-0205-6/FIGURES/8

[32] Watanabe H, Bouazizi M, Ohtsuki T. Hate speech on Twitter: A pragmatic approach to collect hateful and offensive expressions and perform hate speech detection. IEEE Access. 2018;**6**:13825–13835. DOI: 10.1109/ACCESS.2018.2806394

[33] Djuric N, Zhou J, Morris R, Grbovic M, Radosavljevic V, Bhamidipati N, “Hate speech detection with comment embeddings,” in *WWW 2015 Companion - Proceedings of the 24th International Conference on World Wide Web*, Association for Computing Machinery, Inc., May 2015, pp. 29–30. DOI: 10.1145/2740908.2742760

[34] Park JH, Fung P, “One-step and two-step classification for abusive language detection on Twitter,” arXiv Prepr.arXiv1706.01206, pp. 41–45. 2017, [Online]. Available from: http://arxiv.org/abs/1706.01206 [Accessed: 2020-June-04]

[35] A. Shanita Biere Supervisor dr Sandjai Bhulai, “Hate speech detection using natural language processing techniques,” 2018

[36] Njagi D, *et al.* A lexicon-based approach for hate speech detection. International Journal of Multimedia and Ubiquitous Engineering. 2015;**10**(4):215–230. DOI: 10.14257/ijmue.2015.10.4.21

[37] Kumar Sharma H, Singh T, Kshitiz K, Singh H, Kukreja P, “Detecting hate speech and insults on social commentary using NLP and machine learning,” 2017, [Online]. Available from: www.ijetsr.com [Accessed: 2025-June-19]

[38] Varade RS, Pathak VB. Detection of hate speech in Hinglish language. Advances in Intelligent Systems and

Computing. 2020;**1101**:265–276. DOI: 10.1007/978-981-15-1884-3_25

[39] Plaza-Del-Arco FM, Molina-González MD, Ureña-López LA, Martín-Valdivia MT. Detecting misogyny and xenophobia in Spanish tweets using language technologies. ACM Transactions on Internet Technology. 2020;**20**(2). DOI: 10.1145/3369869

[40] Albadi N, Kurdi M, Mishra S, "Are they our brothers? Analysis and detection of religious hate speech in the Arabic Twittersphere," *Proc. 2018 IEEE/ACM Int. Conf. Adv. Soc. Networks Anal. Mining, ASONAM 2018*, pp. 69–76, Oct. 2018, DOI: 10.1109/ASONAM.2018.8508247

[41] Sreelakshmi K, Premjith B, Soman KP. Detection of hate speech text in Hindi-English code-mixed data. Procedia Computer Science. 2020;**171**:737–744. DOI: 10.1016/J.PROCS.2020.04.080

[42] Alfina I, Mulia R, Fanany MI, Ekanata Y. Hate speech detection in the Indonesian language: A dataset and preliminary study. International Conference on Advanced Computer Science and Information Systems (ICACSIS). 2017;**2018**:233–237. DOI: 10.1109/ICACSIS.2017.8355039

[43] Paschalides D, *et al.* MANDOLA: A big-data processing and visualization platform for monitoring and detecting online hate speech. ACM Transactions on Internet Technology. 2020;**20**(2): 1–21. DOI: 10.1145/3371276

[44] Araque O, Iglesias CA. An ensemble method for radicalization and hate speech detection online empowered by Sentic computing. Cognitive Computation. 2022;**14**(1): 48–61. DOI: 10.1007/S12559-021-09845-6/METRICS

[45] Waseem Z, Thorne J, Bingel J. Bridging the Gaps: Multi Task Learning for Domain Transfer of Hate Speech Detection. Cham: Springer; 2018. 29–55 p. DOI: 10.1007/978-3-319-78583-7_3

[46] Del Vigna F, Cimino A, Dell'orletta F, Petrocchi M, Tesconi M, "Hate me, hate me not: Hate speech detection on Facebook," in Ita-sec 17, 2017. [Online]. Available from: https://curl.haxx.se [Accessed: 2020-June-04]

[47] Lynn T, Endo PT, Rosati P, Silva I, Santos GL, Ging D. Data set for automatic detection of online misogynistic speech. Data in Brief. 2019;**26**:104223. DOI: 10.1016/J.DIB.2019.104223

[48] de Gibert O, Pérez N, Pablos AG, Cuadros M. Hate speech dataset from a white supremacy forum. arXiv Prepr. arXiv1809.04444. 2018;11–20. DOI: 10.18653/V1/W18-5102

[49] Ombui E, Karani M, Muchemi L. Annotation Framework for Hate Speech Identification in Tweets: Case Study of Tweets during Kenyan Elections. Nairobi, Kenya: *IST-Africa 2019*. 2019. DOI: 10.23919/ISTAFRICA.2019.8764868

[50] Qian J, Bethke A, Liu Y, Belding E, Wang WY. A benchmark dataset for learning to intervene in online hate speech. EMNLP-IJCNLP 2019 - 2019 Conference on Empirical Methods in Natural Language Processing and 9th International Joint Conference on Natural Language Processing Proceedings of the Conference. 2019;4755–4764. DOI: 10.18653/v1/d19-1482

[51] Wullach T, Adler A, Minkov E. Towards hate speech detection at large via deep generative modeling. IEEE Internet Computing. 2021;**25**(2):48–57. DOI: 10.1109/MIC.2020.3033161

[52] Basak R, Sural S, Ganguly N, Ghosh SK. Online public shaming on Twitter: Detection, analysis, and mitigation. IEEE Transactions on Computational Social Systems. 2019;**6**(2):208–220. DOI: 10.1109/TCSS.2019.2895734

[53] Chen Y, Zhou Y, Zhu S, Xu H, "Detecting offensive language in social media to protect adolescent online safety," *Proc. - 2012 ASE/IEEE Int. Conf. Privacy, Secur. Risk Trust 2012 ASE/IEEE Int. Conf. Soc. Comput. Soc. 2012*, pp. 71–80, 2012, DOI: 10.1109/SOCIALCOM-PASSAT.2012.55

[54] Dinakar K, Jones B, Havasi C, Lieberman H, Picard R. Common sense reasoning for detection, prevention, and mitigation of cyberbullying. ACM Transactions on Interactive Intelligent Systems. 2012;**2**(3):1–30. DOI: 10.1145/2362394.2362400;WGROUP:STRING:ACM

[55] Burnap P, Williams ML. Cyber hate speech on Twitter: An application of machine classification and statistical modeling for policy and decision making. Policy and Internet. 2015;**7**(2):223–242. DOI: 10.1002/poi3.85

[56] Pelzer B, Kaati L, Akrami N, "Directed digital hate," *2018 IEEE Int. Conf. Intell. Secur. Informatics, ISI 2018*, pp. 205–210, Dec. 2018, DOI: 10.1109/ISI.2018.8587396

[57] Lee K, Ram S, "Association for Information Systems Association for Information Systems PERSONA: Personality-based deep learning for detecting hate PERSONA: Personality-based deep learning for detecting hate speech", Available from: https://aisel.aisnet.org/icis2020/hci_artintel/hci_artintel/11 [Accessed: 2025-June-19]

[58] Hosseinmardi H, Mattson SA, Rafiq RI, Han R, Lv Q, Mishra S. Detection of cyberbullying incidents on the Instagram social network. Association for the Advancement of Artificial Intelligence. 2015. Available from: https://arxiv.org/abs/1503.03909v1

[59] Rodriguez A, Argueta C, Chen YL. Automatic detection of hate speech on Facebook using sentiment and emotion analysis. 1st International Conference on Artificial Intelligence in Information and Communication (ICAIIC 2019). 2019;169–174. DOI: 10.1109/ICAIIC.2019.8669073

[60] Ahmad Niam IM, Irawan B, Setianingsih C, Putra BP, "Hate speech detection using latent semantic analysis (LSA) method based on image," *Proc. - 2018 Int. Conf. Control. Electron. Renew. Energy Commun. ICCEREC 2018*, pp. 166–171, Jul. 2018, DOI: 10.1109/ICCEREC.2018.8712111

[61] Miró-Llinares F, Moneva A, Esteve M. Hate is in the air! But where? Introducing an algorithm to detect hate speech in digital microenvironments. Crime Science. 2018;**7**(1):1–12. DOI: 10.1186/S40163-018-0089-1/FIGURES/2

[62] Martins R, Gomes M, Almeida JJ, Novais P, Henriques P, "Hate speech classification in social media using emotional analysis," *Proc. - 2018 Brazilian Conf. Intell. Syst. BRACIS 2018*, pp. 61–66, Dec. 2018, DOI: 10.1109/BRACIS.2018.00019

[63] Gröndahl T, Pajola L, Juuti M, Conti M, Asokan N, "All you need is

'love': Evading hate speech detection," *Proc. ACM Conf. Comput. Commun. Secur.*, pp. 2–12, Oct. 2018, DOI: 10.1145/3270101.3270103;TAXONOMY:TAXONOMY:CONFERENCE-COLLECTIONS;WGROUP:STRING:ACM

[64] Paetzold GH, Malmasi S, Zampieri M, "UTFPR at SemEval-2019 task 5: Hate speech identification with recurrent neural networks," *NAACL HLT 2019 - Int. Work. Semant. Eval. SemEval 2019, Proc. 13th Work.*, pp. 519–523, Apr. 2019, DOI: 10.18653/v1/s19-2093

[65] Mossie Z, Wang JH. Vulnerable community identification using hate speech detection on social media. Information Processing & Management. 2020;**57**(3):102087. DOI: 10.1016/j.ipm.2019.102087

[66] Magu R, Joshi K, Luo J. Detecting the hate code on social media. Proceedings of the International AAAI Conference on Web and Social Media. 2017;**11**(1):608–611. DOI: 10.1609/ICWSM.V11I1.14921

Chapter 4

Petroleum Products' Demand Prediction in Nigeria Based on Machine Learning Tools

Olanrewaju I. Adenekan, Aime Nyoungue and Sophie Hennequin

Abstract

The complex downstream supply chain of the petroleum industry, which encompasses refining, distribution, and marketing, requires strategic and tactical planning for effective product availability and distribution to end users. Accurate demand prediction of petroleum products is strategic to achieving these purposes. In recent years, the industry has experienced a significant transformation driven by digitalization. One of the most significant technological advancements in this context is data analysis facilitated by artificial intelligence, particularly through machine learning (ML) algorithms. ML applications have revolutionized the way companies optimize their operations, enhance safety, reduce costs, and improve overall efficiency. Indeed, good demand forecasting obtained with ML algorithms allows efficient production planning and distribution of petroleum products, and improves customer satisfaction. The objective of this study is to predict the needs for a petroleum product, premium motor spirit, based on real data obtained from the Nigerian petroleum industry. The Nigerian National Petroleum Company (NNPC) has archived historical data related to the production, inventory, and distribution of several petroleum products. Based on these data, we considered four ML algorithms using selected metrics. We also compare the performance of ML models on supply chain performance indexes. The best-performing model(s) are proposed for the prediction of future needs for petroleum products. The knowledge of this forecast is vital for the country's petroleum industry and its stakeholders.

Keywords: demand prediction, machine learning algorithms, data-driven decision-making, Nigerian petroleum industry, supply chain

1. Introduction

Nigeria is a top oil-producing economy in Africa and is considered an emerging economy in the world but faces contrasting scenarios regarding domestic demand for petroleum products. In connection to this, the need for accurate prediction of petroleum products, which is periodically influenced by economic, geopolitical, technological, and social dynamics, has piqued the interest of investors, decision-makers, and other players in the industry. Emerging economies with these dynamics are particularly interested because they are potentially significant players in the industry. Due to these complex interactions, this study has wide appeal to domestic and international actors alike. For close to three decades, the country has exported its crude oil to international markets and imported needed petroleum products for domestic consumption. This has led to increased costs, loss of efficiency, and overall customer dissatisfaction in the supply chain. However, recent developments include the restoration of its refineries by both public and private investors. This development changes the operational arrangements in terms of shifting from importing fuels to domestic production. It also impacts the obligatory crude supply structure to the Organization of the Petroleum Exporting Countries (OPEC). It is crucial to balance domestic and international interests in demand and supply. The recent removal of subsidies on petroleum products disrupts supplier operations and raises the retail price of the product. This affects consumer behavior and poses potential influences on petroleum product demand. Addressing these challenges requires data-driven demand prediction to track consumption accurately, plan production, and effectively distribute products. Accurate demand prediction helps mitigate challenges linked to supply and price volatility, logistics, intermediaries, shareholder crises, and competition from alternative energy sources. It also creates reliable information upstream for transport companies, depots, refineries, and suppliers. Mitigating this complexity among actors improves efficiency, operational costs, and customer satisfaction. Historically, customer data have been computed using traditional statistical models, but these are cumbersome and require a lot of time. The nonlinearity of demand data makes it even more tedious and prone to errors. Alternative methods are found in artificial intelligence (AI) and its applications, such as machine learning (ML), to solve these problems. ML, in recent times, has been supporting research in various fields, including supply chain management (SCM). The algorithms provide complementary or alternative models for decision-making. In this chapter, we present the application of ML algorithms to complement traditional methodologies and address uncertainties in supply chains. While this work helps attain our objectives, it also closes knowledge gaps between researchers and practitioners on the capabilities of ML in SCM. The remainder of this study is organized into sections. Section 2 contains the state-of-the-art connecting ML applications in the supply chain generally. In Section 3, we present the problem description of demand prediction for petroleum products in the Nigerian petroleum industry. This is followed by schematic modeling of the considered system in Section 4. ML tools used for the prediction are briefed in Section 5. Section 6 presents the data collection, preprocessing, and training of our models. Section 7 shows and discusses our results and their applications in the Nigerian petroleum industry, while the conclusion and perspectives of this chapter are drawn in Section 8.

2. Petroleum industry and ML algorithms – a brief state-of-the-art

Generally, the supply chain generates a lot of data from its operations, such as production planning, suppliers' management, inventory management, product transportation and logistics systems, demand and supply forecasting, amongst others [1, 2]. In recent years, ML algorithms have been adopted to create alternative solutions to traditional statistical methods for solving supply chain problems characterized by uncertainties [3–5]. The petroleum industry supply chain is no different and could be considered even more complex compared to other industries. Its operations, divided into upstream, midstream, and downstream, generate voluminous data that could be analyzed and then benefit future activities in a tactical, strategic, and operational manner [6, 7]. ML is a highly regarded tool to investigate data and develop useful models for the industry. Based on real data obtained from the NNPC, demand prediction for petroleum products in Nigeria is possible. Using ML algorithms, the obtained results are applied to optimal production planning, inventory management, and transportation planning. These results help decision-makers and other stakeholders efficiently execute operational and tactical supply chain activities. This work draws inspiration from many applications of ML algorithms to supply chain tactical operations in the petroleum industry and other industries, as highlighted in the next section.

2.1 Tactical applications of ML in supply chain

Transportation is crucial in supply chain distribution and timely delivery for customer satisfaction. ML algorithms' versatility has been applied in critical cases of distribution in SCM.

For effective logistics planning in drug distribution between demand zones in the United States, ML models are used to forecast demand for optimal distribution of insulin. The study compared the performance of random forest (RF), multiple regression, and artificial neural network (ANN). The comparative analysis aids in selecting the most suitable model for the mathematical formulation for optimization [8].

In transportation energy demand, ANN is applied to solve complex nonlinear relationships between energy demand and its effective parameters. It modifies the ANN model's parameters with an improved red fox optimizer (IRFO) to enhance prediction accuracy. The experimental findings validate better performance from the ANN-IRFO model compared to other methods [9].

Also, with ANN, a business model for crude oil transportation is developed alongside other emerging technologies such as cloud computing, automation and robotics, Internet of Things, sensors, mobile devices, and digitization of processes. About 100 ANN tests are performed to predict the economic efficiency performance model, and decisions are made based on the top 5% performance [10].

ML model, long short term memory (LSTM) versatility is used to address logistics problems of diverse, fluctuating customer demand and the complexity of a fully connected supply chain (physical Internet SC). The model is tested with an agricultural supply chain real scenario to assess the performance of a hybrid genetic algorithm and scatter search, and to automate the tuning of the LSTM hyperparameters. In comparison with autoregressive integrated moving average (ARIMA) with exogenous variables, support vector regression (SVR), and multiple linear regression (LR), the LSTM model outperformed the others for continuous fluctuating demand, while the others showed better performance with less varied demand [11].

Furthermore, production planning and scheduling require precise approaches, considering constraints. ML tools enhance the balance of constraints more effectively compared to manual approaches. Storage is expensive and reportedly claims 15–35% of annual business costs, to which recently ML algorithms could help in inventory management cost reduction [5]. To achieve efficiency in these areas, harmony between upstream and downstream actors is essential. This is where ML tools further provide support, as discussed in the following texts.

In [12], ML helps solve and optimize challenges of supplier selection and order allocation versus demand uncertainties. The authors introduced a novel relational regressor chain method for demand forecasting and validated the results with ARIMA and Holt's linear trend, then used the forecasted demand for a multi-objective programming model. Real data from the Canadian food supply network were used to examine the results of demand forecasting and determine the orders allocated to each supplier. These works demonstrated the reliable and efficient performance of ML tools in detecting and reducing hidden inventory along with costs.

Lee, Chou, and Huang [13] proposed a data-driven LSTM-reinforcement learning model for price forecasting and raw material procurement optimization in the petrochemical industry. Using information from upstream and downstream relating to demand and supply rates, the model improved price forecasting and reduced raw material procurement.

Bousqaoui, Slimani, and Achchab [14] carried out a comparative analysis of short-term demand forecast models. They compared ARIMA, a statistical model, and deep learning models, namely multi-layer perceptron, LSTM, and convolutional neural network (CNN), using real data from a Moroccan supermarket. The CNN forecasting performance was the best for solving logistics issues due to its ability to detect the slightest fluctuations in demand patterns.

As an alternative method for qualitative and quantitative demand fluctuation study, Salais-Fierro et al. [15] proposed a soft computing approach of fuzzy logic-ANN. The model integrates predictions generated from expert judgments, historical data, and application in the automotive industry. The result validates the model as a robust and reliable tool for strategic forecasting in manufacturing using time-series data.

Sharma et al. [16] examined different techniques for accurate demand forecasting of natural gas. They evaluated and validated these techniques using real historical consumption and weather forecast data. They considered weather forecasts at six-hour intervals. To capture the intraday variability in demand, they developed a blockwise approach for the forecasting models. Furthermore, they developed four individual prediction models and three ML hybrid models, including ANN algorithms. Strategic decisions were made using ANN-hybrid models because they outperformed others by approximately 15%.

Further tactical applications of ML in the petroleum industry's upstream operations include hydrocarbon production recovery, reservoir systems' resource estimation, and performance analysis.

Citing [17], ML is used in determining hydrocarbon accumulation probability and reserve abundance predictions by using support vector classification and SVR methods.

Al-Rbeawi [18] reviewed the digitalization of the oil and gas industry based on modern approaches, including areas such as exploration and field development; Kuang et al. [6] reviewed drilling and completion, operations, and production emerging methods.

At more strategic levels, ML tools have also played roles in strategic decision-making across industries due to their versatility, as part of effective SCM, addressing the bullwhip effect and enhancing profitability.

In other fields, ML has gained prominence as a tool for organizational strategic planning. For example, Tsilingeridis et al. [19] developed a multidisciplinary framework forecasting tool for the identification of new target markets for elevators and escalators in Europe. They worked with combined LSTM and deep learning network methods using time-series data. Their framework synthesizes profound knowledge of environmental macroeconomics and trending target markets. They proposed an ML model to improve latency demand in computation-intensive and data applications in the industrial Internet of Things. They focused on automatic line scheduling of the Internet of Vehicles, time-sensitive supply chain supervision, and smart control of complex industrial processes.

A. Khan et al. [20] proposed an alternative ANN model to traditional electricity demand forecast models. Their forecast, based on the Cuckoo search algorithm by means of Levy's flight, is found to be operative, efficient, and robust, motivating a new research area within OPEC.

Electricity prices in New Zealand were forecasted by [21] using a hybrid LSTM. With selected features, their model, when compared with the benchmarked model, demonstrated an improved performance of 2–3% with the help of ML models.

ML techniques were applied in petroleum upstream operations for pipeline oil leak detection, classification, prediction, and optimization.

In [22], vector model to achieve higher accuracy in predicting burst pressure. The ML result outperformed traditional empirical methods and benchmark models based on five key performance indicators (KPIs).

Other applications are in predictive analytics to assess pipeline integrity and management in oil and gas transportation [23, 24].

With LSTM and time-delay neural network models, they mitigated the overfitting problem.

ML has also been used for sustainability and promoting alternative fuels in combination with other methods. For example, Momenitabar et al. [25] worked to design a bioethanol supply chain with methods combining ML techniques such as RF, extreme gradient boost, and ensemble learning to forecast demand. They considered the best data input method for the proposed mathematical formulation used for strategic planning and tactical decision variables. Their work shows how integral ML models are beneficial to emerging technologies. Trending research areas such as carbon storage corresponding to sustainability have also applied ML methods for underground storage optimization. An example is the work done using ANNs to train datasets from historical databases to develop a proxy model, which was optimized with existing methods to achieve set objectives. ML methods' invaluable usefulness to modern research is also found in production prediction and energy saving for complex chemical processes.

Machine learning tools are also used in port operations [26], electric vehicle diagnostics, and battery performance. Also, in inflation forecasting, new contenders were compared to classical models. Data-driven probabilistic ML methods for smart energy systems and blockchain applications in the oil and gas industry, as discussed in **Table 1,** present different types of ML algorithms proposed by the authors.

ML algorithms' suitability for a data-driven industry such as the petroleum supply chain is filled with huge prospects to bridge gaps. Existing literature on SCM operations in production planning, inventory management, and transportation are well-documented research areas of benefit. Therefore, our study would apply ML to address critical uncertainties in the petroleum supply chain. We propose to predict

Refinery	Capacity (bpd)	Capacity barrels per year (bpy)	Status (operating %)	Location
Warri Refinery and Petrochemical Complex	125,000	45,625,000	Active: 60%	Ekpan, Warri, Delta State (south–south)
Kaduna Refinery and Petrochemical Complex	110,000	40,150,000	In progress	Kaduna, Kaduna State (northwest)
Port Harcourt Refinery and Petrochemical Complex	Old: 60,000 New: 150,000	Old: 21,900,000 New: 54,750,000	Old active: 60% New: under rehabilitation	Alesa Eleme, Rivers State (south–south)
Dangote Refinery	650,000	237,250,000	Active	Lekki, Lagos (southwest)
OPAC Refinery, Delta State (Modular)	10,000	3,650,000	Active	Kwale, Delta State (south–south)
Walter Smith Refinery	5,000 (expandable 50,000)	1,825,000	Active	Ibigwe, Imo State (southeast)
Duport Midstream	2,500	912,500	Active	Egboko, Edo State (south–south)
BUA Petrochemical Refinery	200,000	73,000,000	Planned	Akwa-Ibom State (south–south)
Edo Refinery And Petrochemical Company	2,500	252,000	Completed	Ikpoba-Okha, Edo State (south–south)
Niger Delta Petroleum Refinery	11,000	4,015,000	Active	Ogbele, Rivers State (south–south)
Azikel Refinery	12,000	4,380,000	Under construction	Yenagoa, Bayelsa State (south–south)
Atlantic International Refinery	2,000	730,000	Under construction	Brass, Bayelsa State (south–south)

Table 1.
Refineries in Nigeria.

the demand for premium motor spirit (PMS) based on a 92-day dataset and compare the performances of ML algorithms as applicable to the Nigerian petroleum industry. Demand prediction is important for the Nigerian petroleum industry, which is faced with diverse uncertainties; these problems are discussed in the next section.

3. Problem descriptions of the Nigerian petroleum industry

Nigeria is among the top 15 oil- and gas-producing countries and a member of OPEC. However, the Nigerian petroleum industry faces multiple uncertainties. The primary challenge is the long-term redundancy or underutilization of refineries for almost three decades. This peculiarity makes Nigeria import petroleum products up to 96% of its consumption [27]. It is also responsible for volatility in petroleum product pricing, supply, and distribution. This method creates high operational costs and increasing inventory costs from dead stock occupying more than 6% of storage capacity. Other challenges include delays, product theft and diversion, crude pipeline vandalism, and policy somersaults. These challenges are amplified by a long chain of actors and intermediaries, creating more uncertainties in the network. The data from the national inventory indicate sometimes irreconcilable variances in product supply and distribution. In all, this arrangement constitutes inefficiencies and high overall costs.

Recent developments in the Nigerian petroleum industry include the construction of new refineries and the reconstruction of old ones. One of them is the Dangote Refinery, with a capacity of 650,000 barrels per day (bpd), which commenced operations in January 2024. Two public refineries, with total capacities of 275,000 bpd, have also been restored but are operating at partial capacity (**Table 1**). This implies that domestic consumption would be satisfied from local production, with opportunities to export the surplus. Other refineries are in progress and will further increase the surplus when ready. It is safe to say that Nigeria is transitioning the petroleum industry from redundant refineries to overflowing production, thus making it imperative to accurately estimate real-time daily consumption. This will help determine buffer stocks and exportation opportunities, leading to improved efficiency and costing. PMS is Nigeria's highest-consuming petroleum product, estimated at 68 million liters per day in 2022 by the NNPC. It dominates market consumption in Nigeria because of its wide usage in transportation and other strategic sectors of the economy. Data estimate PMS as 72% of the daily petroleum products consumption. Automotive gas oil and aviation turbine kerosene account for 21% and 5%, respectively. Dual-purpose kerosene for domestic cooking is 1%, while base oil, low pour fuel oil, and bitumen, as shown in **Figure 1,** make up the remaining portion. In 2023, there was a constant reduction averaging 26.5% every quarter in PMS consumption. This anomaly is strange and requires proper attention, especially with the transition from importing to production, for proper planning. In this chapter, we focus on the prediction of PMS because of its importance and the challenges associated with data on other products.

Table 1 highlights the state petroleum refineries in Nigeria. The details provided for each refinery include design capacity for daily production, annual production, state of operation, and locations within the country. With the known design

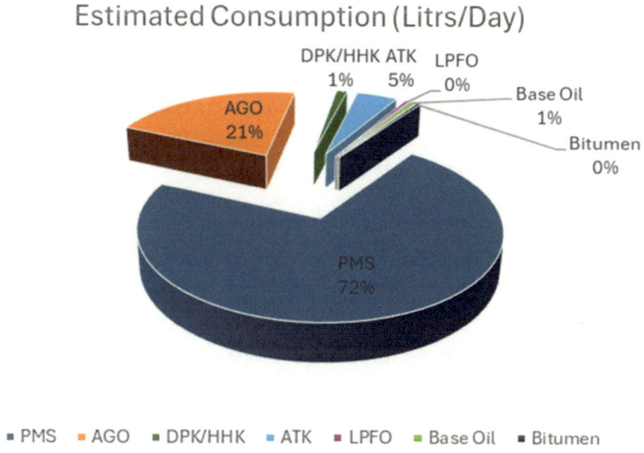

Figure 1.
Estimated daily consumption of petroleum products in Nigeria.

capacity, we can estimate expected daily production. The working state and active production capacity provide actual volumes produced per day. Further details, such as other products, are essential to further ascertain definite values for each of them. The information about refinery locations gives state and regional details, both of which would be useful in discussing our results. Considering the working refineries, 694,500 bpd of crude oil are processed daily. Dangote Refinery, operating at 85% working capacity, processes 79.5% of the total, amounting to 552,500 bpd. The public refineries account for 15%, producing 111,000 bpd, while the remaining 5.5% is shared among the five modular refineries in operation. It is worth noting that the information emphasizes crude oil production. The product types are not detailed in the table; however, the products are based on the designs of the fractional distiller, which vary from one refinery to another. Nevertheless, the information is highly relevant for understanding the relationship between demand, production, and suppliers of crude oil. Additionally, this chapter focuses on PMS demand prediction, which we highlighted after **Table 1**.

In summary, the need for accurate demand prediction of gasoline is highlighted as follows:

- Nigeria imports petroleum products for domestic consumption.
- Uncertainties and intermediaries often disrupt products' supply chain.
- New and restored refineries hugely boost local production.
- The refineries capacities are still underutilized.
- The transition requires accurate demand prediction for efficiency and improved costing.
- It will help with proper resource allocation in strategic areas such as storage.
- It will create a sufficient buffer and meet external obligations and exporting opportunities.
- It will mitigate dead stock emerging from overstocking (~6% for PMS).

To achieve the stated objective, it is necessary to understand the product and information flow within the supply chain. In the next section, we present a schematic explanation, including the actors and consumers.

4. Schematic model of the considered supply chain

The previous model of importing products starts operation from the stock-receiving ports (Apapa, Lagos handling more than 70%), where trucks are loaded for distribution. For farther customer reach, some products are transported to inland depots via pipeline. It also fairly reduces congestion at the port. Information on demand is organized by states; thus, the products are dispatched on a state basis. To replace that model with a transition to domestic production, we propose a new system in **Figure 2**.

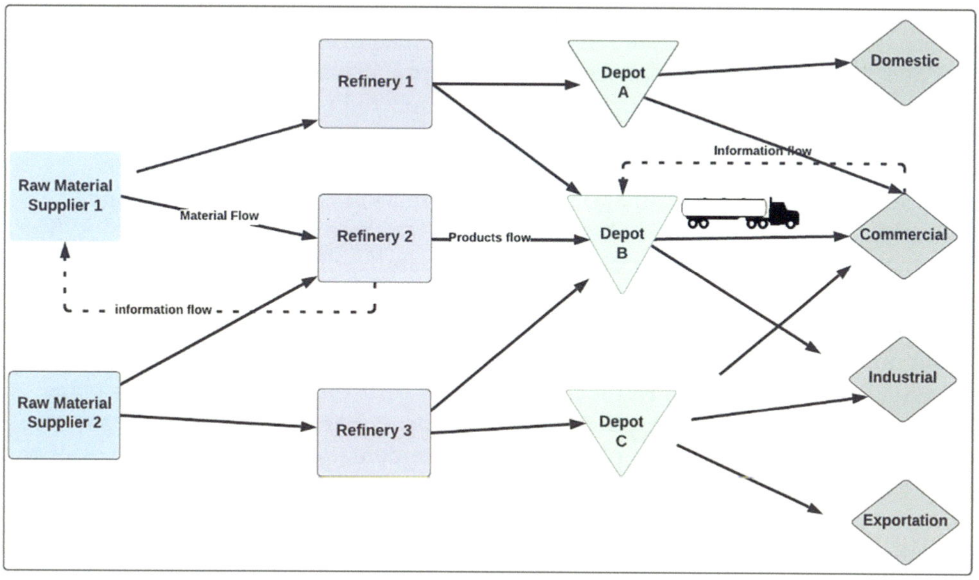

Figure 2.
Considered petroleum supply chain.

The considered scheme highlights some of the features in recent developments. The highlights are stated as follows:

- Predefined and fixed locations for the refineries, depots, and customers.
- Demand for products is directly related to production planning at the refinery and inventory safety stocks.
- Different customers are allowed to be served by different distributors based on product availability and proximity.
- The product's demand is mostly known over a period. However, there could be a surge in demand, which could have a short-term effect on the distribution.
- We aggregate modular refineries' outputs as one because of proximity.
- Historical trucks-out/supply data are our demand data for this work.
- The ML models for demand prediction provide useful data to plan production at the refineries, including the allocation of production quotas based on locations and prevailing demands, to avoid overproduction or underproduction of petroleum products.

The schematic in **Figure 2** represents our considered supply chain. It comprises suppliers at node 1, refineries at node 2, depots/warehouses at node 3, and customers at node 4. The previous importation model only included node 3 and node 4 because the refineries were redundant. It also features transport modes for products. The importation model only uses trucks because 96% of products are transported via trucks. In our considered model, the suppliers transport crude oil to the refineries via pipeline, while other materials necessary for production are shipped. The refining operation is carried out, and products are transported to tank farms or depots. The trucks then load the products en route to the customers. These customers are classified into industrial, commercial, and retail categories. This customer classification provides definite consumer information compared to demand generalized under states. We also create room for the exportation of surplus. The information backflow implies customer's requests/feedback, which are communicated to the depots or loading points. This information, archived over a period, forms the basis for predicting customers' requests. The information helps to maintain optimal stock levels. The inventory actors use this information to manage requests sent to producing refineries. With this information, the refinery plans production and manages suppliers' relationships. Other external factors may also influence these decisions; the more accurate the demand prediction, the better the supply chain decisions for efficiency and cost management. Our model is better suited to operate the transitioning in the Nigerian industry, which is linked to new and functional refineries. However, the data for our work are taken from the importation model to be used with ML applications. In the next section, we describe some ML models, their limitations, and applications. With this information, we have different options to work with and select suitable ones for our application.

5. Machine learning tools

Machine learning is a subset of AI. The availability of high-performance computers makes it possible to process huge datasets to obtain useful outcomes. ML, in principle, enables systems to learn from historical data and improve predictions or decisions without explicit programming. Crude oil refining, distribution, retailing, and other downstream operations generate huge datasets that employ ML for data-driven decision-making, predictive analytics, and process optimization. Complex datasets involving demand volatility, logistics inefficiencies, and sustainability pressures are ideal situations where ML is applicable. In this work, ML is used in demand prediction of petroleum products using real data to determine future needs for the products. In **Table 2**, we describe some known ML models, their applications in the petroleum industry, and their limitations.

We consider the information in **Table 2** adequate to apply ML algorithms in this work. Its suitability for a data-driven industry like the petroleum supply chain, with huge prospects to bridge research gaps, is unprecedented. We have well-documented literature on research areas of benefits, including SCM.
Machine learning requires data collection, preprocessing, and model training to execute its operations. The next section explains our data collection, limitations, and preprocessing based on a 92-day dataset from one of the industry actors in Nigeria.

6. Data collection and preprocessing

Forecasting the future demand for petroleum products requires that relevant data be provided. The proposed study deals with real cases of demand for

Model	Description	Limitations	Applications	References
ANN	Inspired by the human brain, with the capability to analyze complex, nonlinear data and uncover hidden patterns to make predictions. Superior convergence rate and flexible architecture for various tasks.	Prone to overfitting with small datasets, requiring heavy computational resources and extensive data pre-processing, and easily trapped in local optima.	Supply chain optimization, fuel consumption forecasting, price prediction, energy comparative analysis.	[8, 9, 28, 29]
Decision tree (DT)	A tree-based model that splits data into branches for interpretable decisions. Can handle both numerical and categorical datasets, and can manage missing values.	Unstable with small data changes, leading to poor generalization. Difficult to control tree size; highly prone to sampling error.	Enhanced oil recovery, drug response prediction, weather forecasting, and customer segmentation.	[22, 30]
Linear regression (LR)	Models the linear relationship between the dependent variable and one or more independent variables by fitting a linear equation. It is highly interpretable and easy to implement.	Assumes linearity, which may oversimplify complex data. Sensitive to outliers and multicollinearity, leading to biased results.	Natural gas demand forecasting, oil production forecasting, predictive maintenance.	[14, 31, 32]
Support vector machine (SVM)	A classification model that finds an optimal hyperplane with superior mathematical tractability to separate data, effective for high-dimensional datasets. It is suitable for binary classification with good accuracy.	Requires optimization of kernel and regularization hyperparameters. Computationally intensive for large datasets. Unsuitable for imbalanced datasets.	Natural gas resource evaluation and prediction, analysis of fossil fuel consumption, logistics demand forecasting, risk assessment, supplier segmentation, and production planning.	[17, 28, 30, 33]
K-nearest neighbor	A simple, nonparametric algorithm that classifies data based on the majority class of its k-nearest neighbors. It is flexible and effective for multi-class problems.	Computationally expensive for large datasets due to distance calculations. Sensitive to irrelevant features and requires feature scaling.	Pipeline anomaly detection, big petroleum data analytics, prediction, demand forecasting, oil pipeline performance analysis.	[30, 34]
LSTM	A type of recurrent neural network designed to capture long-term temporal dependencies in sequential data, achieving high accuracy for time-series tasks.	Slow training occurs due to sequential processing. It requires large amounts of data and computational resources and is less flexible for nonsequential tasks.	Natural gas pipeline simulation, electricity demand forecasting.	[11, 30, 35]
Ensemble learning	Combines multiple models (weak and strong learners) to improve prediction accuracy and robustness over single models.	High computational cost and complexity in tuning multiple models may lead to overfitting if not properly managed.	Pipeline corrosion rate prediction, burst pressure prediction.	[36, 37]

Model	Description	Limitations	Applications	References
Graph neural network	Models that leverage graph-based data representations capture complex, nonlinear relationships in networked data, enhancing decision-making for structured data.	High computational cost, especially for large graphs. Requires expertise to design graph structures.	Transportation route optimization, natural gas pipeline design and characterization, logistics network planning.	[32, 38]

Table 2.
A synthesis of selected ML models' applications in the petroleum industry.

petroleum products in Nigeria. We use data from the archive of the Nigerian Midstream Downstream Petroleum Regulatory Authority (NMDPRA). The types of data include daily trucks-out in truck numbers and volumes supplied. We also have inventory management data with stock received, dispatched, and balance for eight products. The data also contain daily sufficiency but do not indicate customers' destinations. Only the PMS daily trucks-out data include the destination of the trucks. This makes it suitable to be used as demand or requests from each of the 37 states in Nigeria. With the data, we face challenges of data breakage between months. While other products' daily trucks-out data were not available, the available PMS data feature breakage in between. This limits our useful data to spread across a few months without breakage. We obtained the most recent consistent data as reported, which covers May–July 2023. The trucks-out data represent demand due to direct correlation with customers' requests. Trucks-out details of other petroleum products are not available besides the total daily evacuations from the depots and the estimated national daily consumption for the products. Therefore, our study could not predict demand per state for those products.

During data collection efforts made to obtain more data from primary sources, we faced obstacles due to data classification and protection bureaucracy. As a result, we made use of limited data, consistent over 92 days between the months of May and July 2023, obtained from the website of the NMDPRA. We tried to prepare the data in a creative way to showcase some groundbreaking applications. In the next section, we present the preprocessing of our data.

6.1 Data preprocessing

In this work, the data available are detailed with daily information on trucks-out numbers and volumes dispatched to 37 states, including the Federal Capital Territory (FCT) in Nigeria. For the complete study, we propose to aggregate daily supplies into weekly, monthly, or annual supplies to each state using the truck numbers and volumes. This approach will be helpful in this context because these aggregated data are easier to relate to in production and inventory management. We also attempted to present the data in the form of geopolitical locations in Nigeria. The reason for this is that the refinery's location makes geopolitical details more interesting and practical in the real world. However, the sparsely available data limit this approach. Therefore, the method used involves selecting individual states and their corresponding data as output variable targets for machine learning (ML) training, testing, and predictions. In the event of this study, this option includes daily truck dispatches and volumes to individual states over the course of 92 days.

6.2 Model trainings

We trained and tested four models on one set of observed time-series data – ANN, DT, LR, and SVM. We used MATLAB's Regression Learner app on our 92-day dataset of PMS truck-outs, installed on a standard laptop, Dell Latitude 5520 (Processor: 11th Gen Intel(R) Core(TM) i7-1165G7 @ 2.80 GHz 1.69 GHz, RAM: 16GB). We selected the models to balance between standard regression techniques (DT, LR) and advanced methods (ANN, SVM) to capture nonlinearity, enhancing the study's methodology with multiple approaches. The dataset was split into 70% (64 days) for training and 30% (27 days) for testing in the sequence of the days.

ANN is a tri-layered network (input, 10-neuron hidden layer, output). It leverages multiple hyperparameters with a sigmoid activation function (rate 0.01) and 1,000 epochs to adapt to the nonlinearity features of the data and ensure convergence that simpler models might miss. The Levenberg–Marquardt method is used for the backpropagation algorithm and efficiency with small datasets. Our ANN set up this, but we adapt the epoch count to smaller datasets, unlike the larger insulin demand series in [8]. We chose a DT of fine tree with a maximum depth of 5 to contain overfitting observed in the earlier test with extended growth. The growth is from randomly drawn samples from the learning base combined with several predictions from each DT to induce a more accurate and stable prediction by the algorithm. The number of trees to build is one of the most important parameters of the RF algorithm. This algorithm allows overcoming the problem of overfitting on top of the data that occurs in DT algorithms. LR is a type of supervised ML algorithm that assumes a linear relationship between dependent variables and one or more independent features by fitting a linear equation to observed data. The simplicity, interpretability, and easy implementation of LR are notable strengths. This model is suitable for predictions in cases where responses are numerical [39]. SVM used a linear kernel, optimized via MATLAB's default quadratic solver. SVM is a popular model used in many pieces of literature to predict time-series data in supply chains, including customer demand. A SVM uses hyperplanes to classify data. The SVM computes the equation of the hyperplane that divides the dataset into classes.

MATLAB's layout is structured into learning, testing, and explanation windows. To initiate a session on the regression learner application, data are imported into the workspace or taken from spreadsheets stored on the network or local computer for training. The data are classified into predictors and response. We tune the percentage of data for training and testing, as well as the hyperparameters for each model, to obtain satisfying outputs. Depending on the selection, we have the option to sort for favorites or evaluation metrics. The same process is repeated for testing. We have our results with some metric information, which explains the models' performances. The model can be exported to the MATLAB workspace for prediction using other data. In what follows, we present the results and application to a real-world scenario.

7. ML algorithms, results, and discussion

In this section, we present the results for the four tested ML models from our experiment. The corresponding figures for each model are also presented thereafter.

In **Table 3,** the values are presented for the number of trucks and volumes in liters demanded for PMS by 37 states, including the FCT. The evaluation metrics include mean absolute error (MAE), mean square error (MSE), root mean square error (RMSE), mean absolute percentage error (MAPE), and R^2. These details are presented in **Table 3** and briefly discussed thereafter. We also present the graphics for the predictions against the observed values. What follows are the notes on evaluation metrics for the models. To evaluate the performance of ML models in comparing actual values to predicted values, we consider the following metrics.

MAE calculates the average difference between the predicted values and the actual values. It is also known as scale-dependent accuracy, as it calculates error in observations taken on the same scale. It is used as an evaluation metric for regression models in ML to predict the accuracy of the ML model.

$$MAE = \frac{1}{T}\sum_{i=1}^{T}|y_t - \hat{y}_t| \tag{1}$$

where

T is the number of tested steps,

y_t is the observed value, and

$\hat{y}_t$ is the predicted value.

MSE is the mean of the square of the differences between the actual values and the predicted values.

$$MSE = \sum\frac{(y_t - \hat{y}_t)^2}{T} \tag{2}$$

Models	Sets	MAE	MSE	RMSE	MAPE	R^2
		Trucks number/ volume	**Trucks number/ volume**	**Trucks number/ volume**	**Trucks number/ volume**	**Trucks number/ volume**
LR	Train	17.74/6.90e05	747.33 /8.20e11	27.34/9.06e05	80.4%/78.6%	0.45/0.62
	Test	1.29e–14/ 4.11e05	5.5043e–28/ *2.76e-19*	2.351e–14/ 5.25e-10	0.00%/0.00%	1.00/1.00
Tri-layered neural network	Train	7.89/7.96e05	128.03/1.32e12	18.20/1.15e06	33.7%/69.2%	0.75/0.4
	Test	0.0008/ 0.1142	9.66e–7/ 0.020305	0.00099/ 0.1425	0.0%/0.00%	1.00/1.00
Linear SVM	Train	9.80/3.65e05	96.12/2.04e11	9.80/4.51e11	32.5%/37.1%	0.93/0.91
	Test	3.52/1.55e05	12.43/4.37e10	3.52/2.09e05	13.8%/18.4%	0.99/0.98
DT (fine)	Train	18.42/6.55e10	1242.9/1.74e12	35.26/1.32e06	75.3%/52.9%	0.08/0.20
	Test	8.76/3.57e05	533.06/8.30e11	23.09/9.12e05	21.8%/20.6%	0.58/0.61

Table 3.
Results for the applied ML models.

RMSE squares the prediction differences to place an even stronger emphasis on the discrepancies between the predictions and the observed values.

$$RMSE = \sqrt{\frac{1}{T}\sum_{i=1}^{T}(y_t - \hat{y}_t)^2} \tag{3}$$

R^2 reveals the correlation between the actual dependent variable and the forecasted dependent variable and measures the accuracy of a model in explaining the variance associated with the variables, to be interpreted based on the explicative variables.

We also use, as a metric for the neural network, the *R*-value that is the coefficient of correlation. It shows how well the predicted outputs match the real outputs when we train the network. A network's performance is considered good if *R* tends to 1. Otherwise, we should train our network with other parameters, such as the number and size of hidden layers, or check the input parameters again.

In each figure below, the x-axis represents each state in the country of reference, while the y-axis represents the demands. The blue markers indicate the actual values, while the predicted values are represented by the yellow markers. For each model, we have stated earlier that 90% of the data are used for training and the remaining 10% for testing.

7.1 Linear regression

In **Figures 3** and **4**, the relationship between actual and predicted values for the LR model is presented. It shows the next day's number of trucks predicted to be dispatched to each state and the corresponding volumes. From observation, the predictions show a wide range of characteristics, especially in sensitive states. For example, in the 25th state, which is the peak point on the graph and considered the economic hub of the country, the demand for both trucks and volumes is near perfectly predicted. In other states, which also have economic importance and fall among the top 10 states in demand, the disparity is characterized by noticeable underpredictions and overpredictions. The variance in prediction is characterized by positive and negative inconsistencies. For example, the 20th state has an overprediction in trucks by 180%, while the equivalent volume is underpredicted by 300%. State 28 also has an interesting feature, which marks a perfect number of trucks but a 200% overpredicted volume. Aside from that, there were too many misalignments in demand, which is not good for the planning of production and inventory.

Although there are many overprediction, the model prediction for point *25* is good considering its importance in the scheme of things. The linear regression MAE values for training and tested data are 17.741 and 1.2939×10^{-14} for trucks and 6.9020×10^{05} and 4.1139×10^{05} for volumes, respectively. The results for MSE, RMSE, MAPE, and R^2 values are 747.33, 27.337, 80.4%, and 0.45 for training and 5.5043×10^{-28}, 2.3461×10^{-14}, 0.00%, and 1.00 for tested data on trucks, respectively. The metric values for volumes are highlighted in **Table 3**. The performance is a combination of positive and negative data. The negatives are profound compared to the positives. This model is well noted and compared to other models for decision-making.

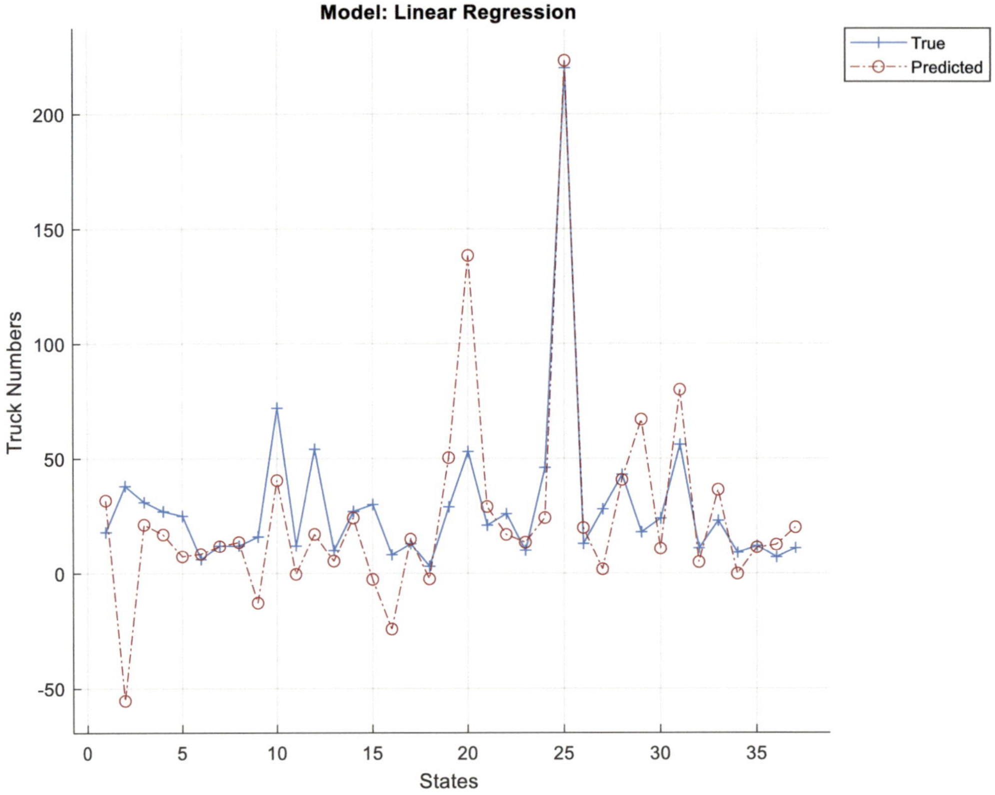

Figure 3.
Linear regression: States vs. trucks demand.

7.2 Artificial neural network

Figures 5 and **6** represent neural network results for the demand by trucks and volumes for each state. There are more cases of close values between actual and predicted values. The state with the highest demand has an average of about 25% for trucks and volumes, which is high compared to the LR model. This 25% average for this state is not too much of a concern because demand would make it disappear in a shorter time compared to other states. However, the model's performance across other states shows closer predictions to the actual values.

The actual-to-predicted values for trucks are more consistent except for the 15th and 25th states. The values for the volumes are alike for 15th and 25th states, but most values are underpredicted and close. The neural network model performance metrics for trucks are MAE, MSE, RMSE, MAPE, and R^2, with values of 7.89, 128.03, 11.315, 33.7%, and 0.9 for trained data and 0.00075, 9.66×10^{-7}, 0.00098, 0.0%, and 1.00 for tested data.

7.3 Support vector machine

In **Figures 7** and **8**, the SVM models show and maintain a close margin between the actual and predicted marker for the demands both by trucks and by

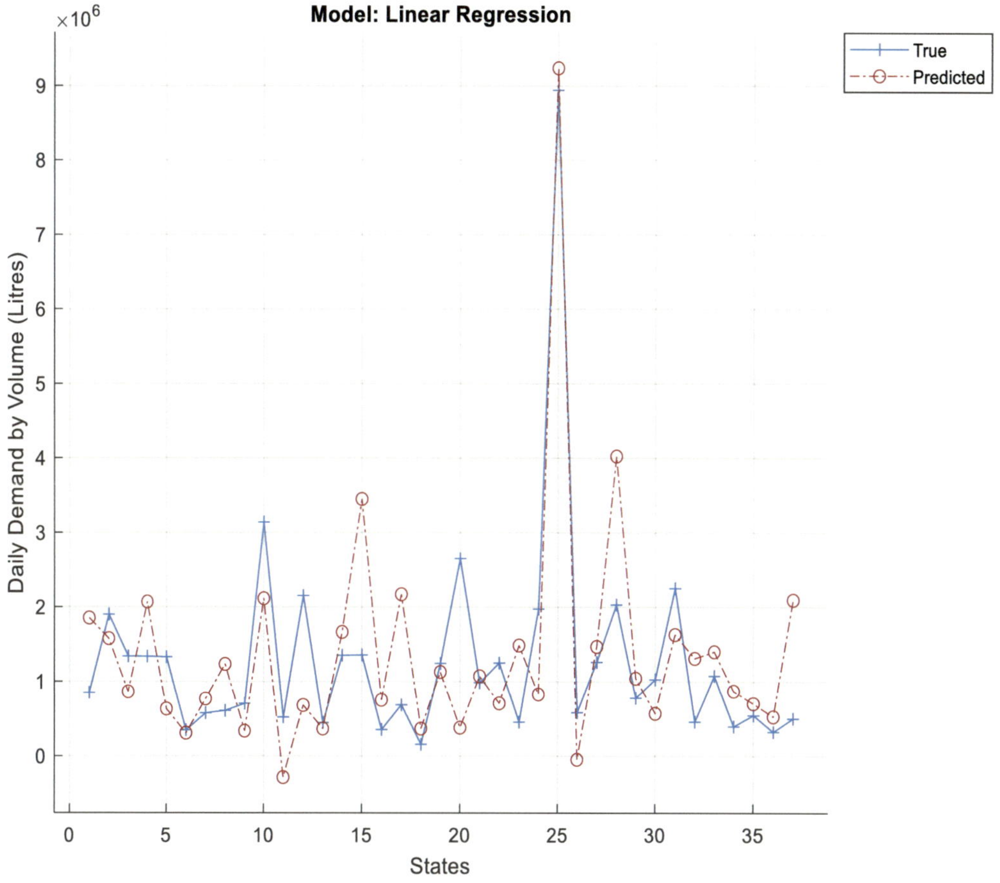

Figure 4.
Linear regression: States vs. volumes demand.

volumes. There are many minimal close margins of overprediction between the values. The model shows best performance in both instances. Considering the 15th and 25th states, the model prediction variance is less than $\pm 2.5\%$ which is good.

This prediction is better for the neural network, which has been the overall better performer. The SVM comparison to other models also shows a close value in trained and tested data, with corresponding values of 9.8042, 96.123, 9.8042, 32.5%, and 0.93 in the previous order for trained data, and 3.5252, 12.427, 3.5252, 13.8%, and 0.99 for tested data. The result is the best fit considering the graphics and metrics presented in **Table 3** for trucks and volume demands.

7.4 Decision tree

Figures 9 and **10** show the plot for the DTs. The results, specifically in the 25th state, are too underpredicted for both trucks and volumes. The same happened with the 10th, 15th, 27th, 28th, and 37th states. The predictions at these determinant points are very poor and unreliable for adoption when compared to other models.

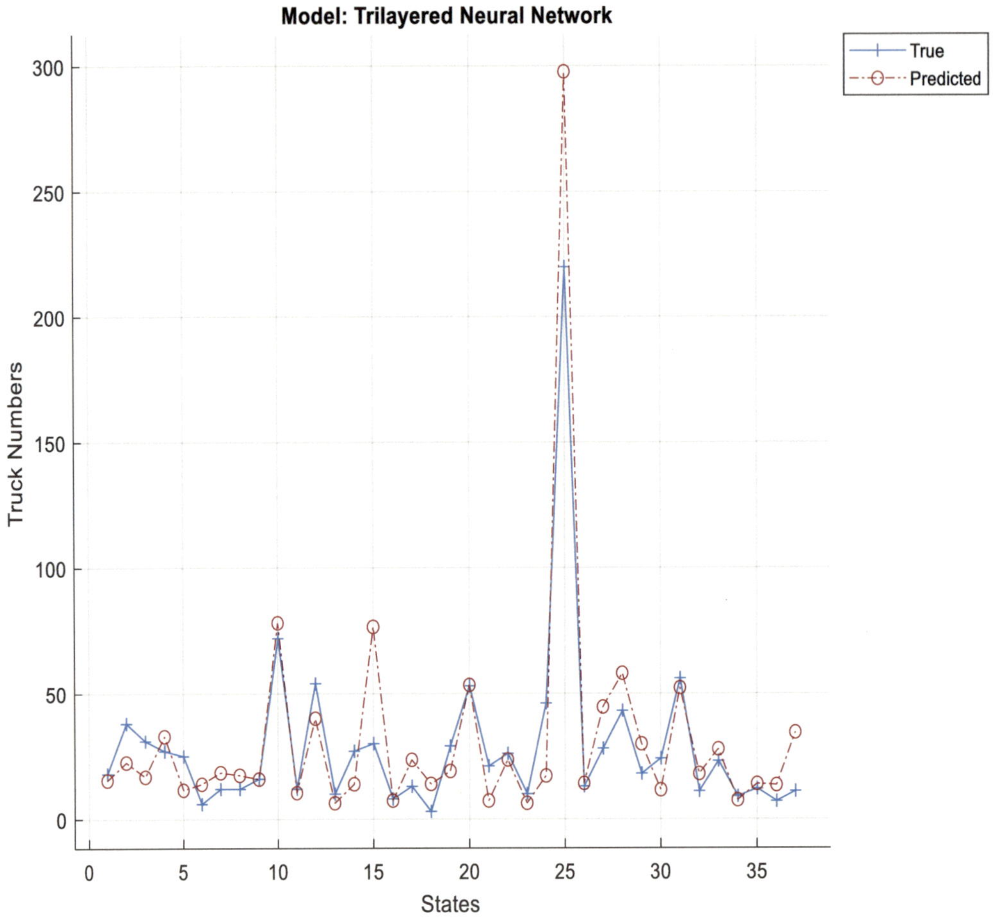

Figure 5.
ANN: States vs. truck demand.

Based on the metrics, particularly RMSE performance, the lowest value justifies how good the performance of both the neural network and SVM models is. The SVM model's overall performance, as enumerated, shows a more consistent performance across the board with the neural network and is a highly rated pick for demand forecasting in our study based on RMSE values. The neural network model performed closely and is considered worthy of adoption. For both the training and testing phases, the performances of the NN and SVM models are competitive, as presented in **Table 3**. The two models could be combined in usage for the best results. The performance of the LR and medium DT models is understandably at a larger variance. This possibility could be traced to the nonlinearity of the data used for our experiments.

Table 4 lists KPIs rated on a scale of 1–5 to evaluate how ML models enhance decision-making in SCM. Lower values of metrics such as MAE, MAPE, and RMSE indicate better performance. Overpredictions and underpredictions also influence ratings. **Table 4** shows the impacts of LR, ANN, DT, and SVM on selected KPIs.

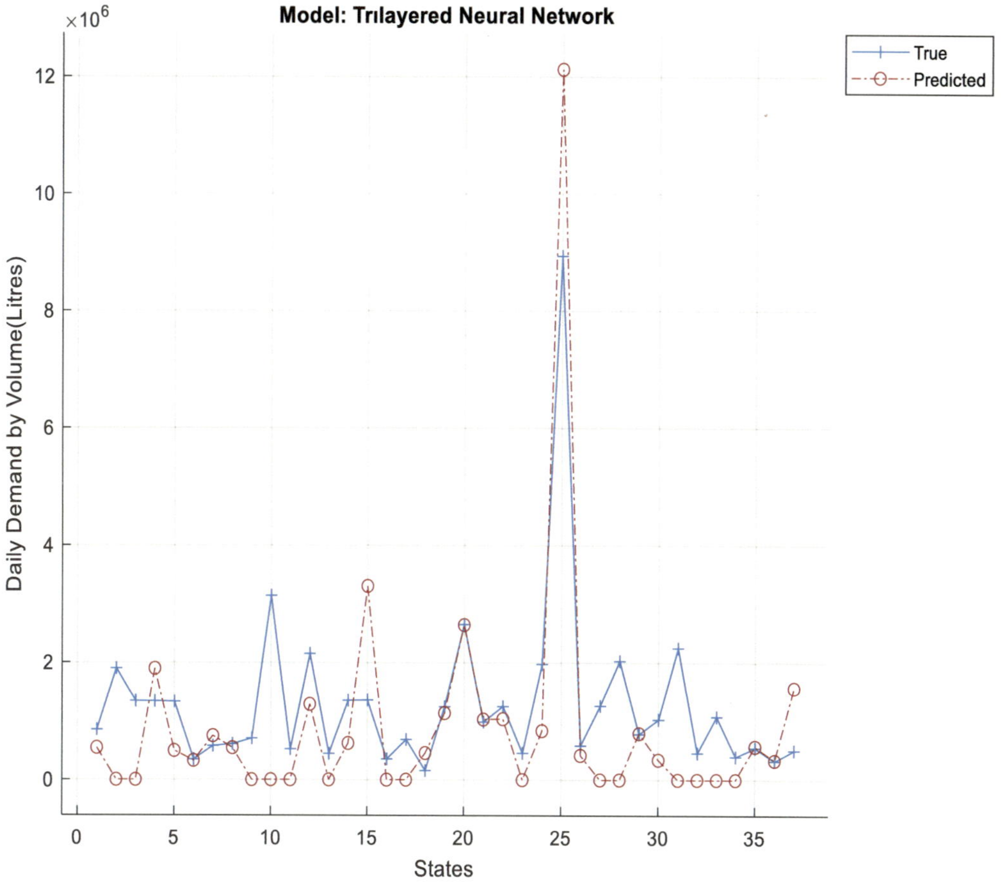

Figure 6.
ANN: States vs. volume demand.

The ratings based on performances are interpreted in a manner of impact on the KPIs.

i. Inventory management

Based on MAE, RMSE, and MAPE values, ANN and SVM (rating - 5) models outperformed LR and DT (rating - 3), enabling accuracy in demand forecasting. This reduces overstocking and understocking, directly lowers carrying and stock-out costs, and improves resource allocation and customer satisfaction due to product availability.

ii. Production planning and scheduling

ANN and SVM's superior MAE, MAPE, and RMSE align production with demand, minimizing underproduction and overproduction risks. They optimize resource use, labor, and batch sizes, reducing waste and costs. LR's negative values and DT's variability are less reliable, while ANN and SVM enhance agility and safety stock management.

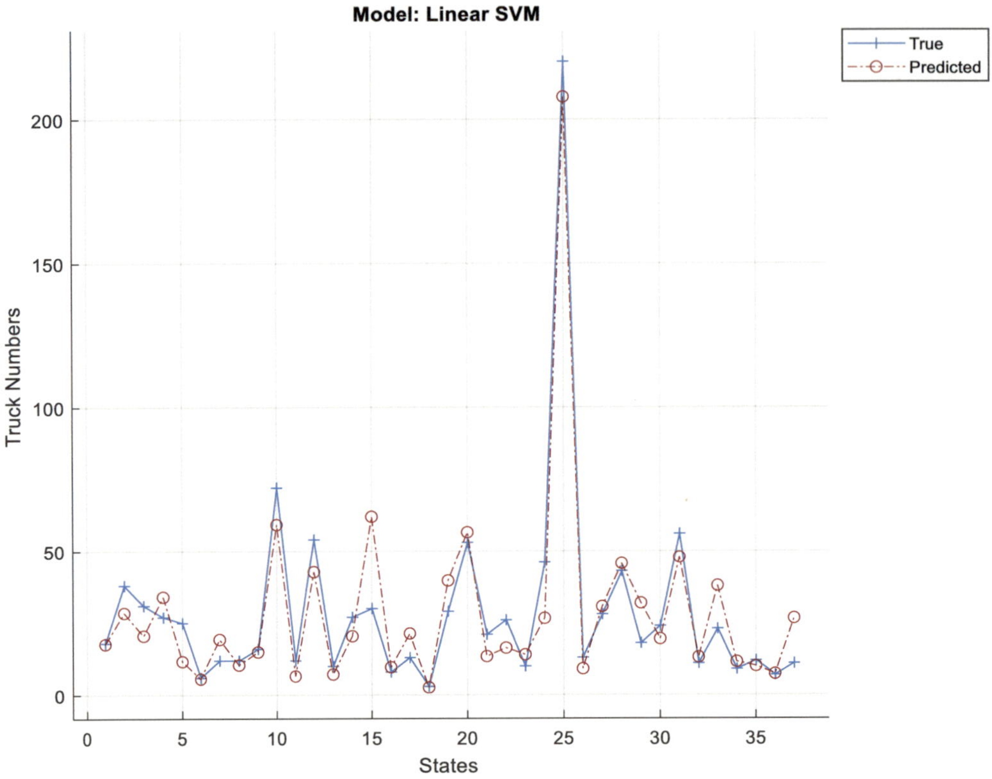

Figure 7.
SVM: States vs. demand trucks.

iii. Localized decision, transportation, pipeline, and refinery utilization

ANN and SVM's accurate forecasts support nodal decisions in inventory, refinery optimization, and transportation. They improve route planning, load optimization, and maintenance scheduling, reducing fuel and carrying costs. LR and DT's lower accuracy limits data-driven decisions, affecting the overall resilience of the supply chain.

iv. Procurement, supplier relationships, lead time sensitivity, and financial planning

High-performing ANN and SVM (based on MSE, MAPE, RMSE) streamline procurement and supplier coordination with 90% demand accuracy. This ensures timely raw material orders, fosters strong supplier relationships, optimizes lead times, and aligns financial planning with production needs. The refinery can plan the proper product mix to satisfy different customers.

v. Marketing and sales, and customer's satisfaction

ANN and SVM's precise demand forecasts align marketing and sales with upstream activities, minimizing effort and boosting customer satisfaction. They enhance resource allocation, operational efficiency, and increase revenue and return on investments through better sales opportunities, unlike less accurate LR and DT.

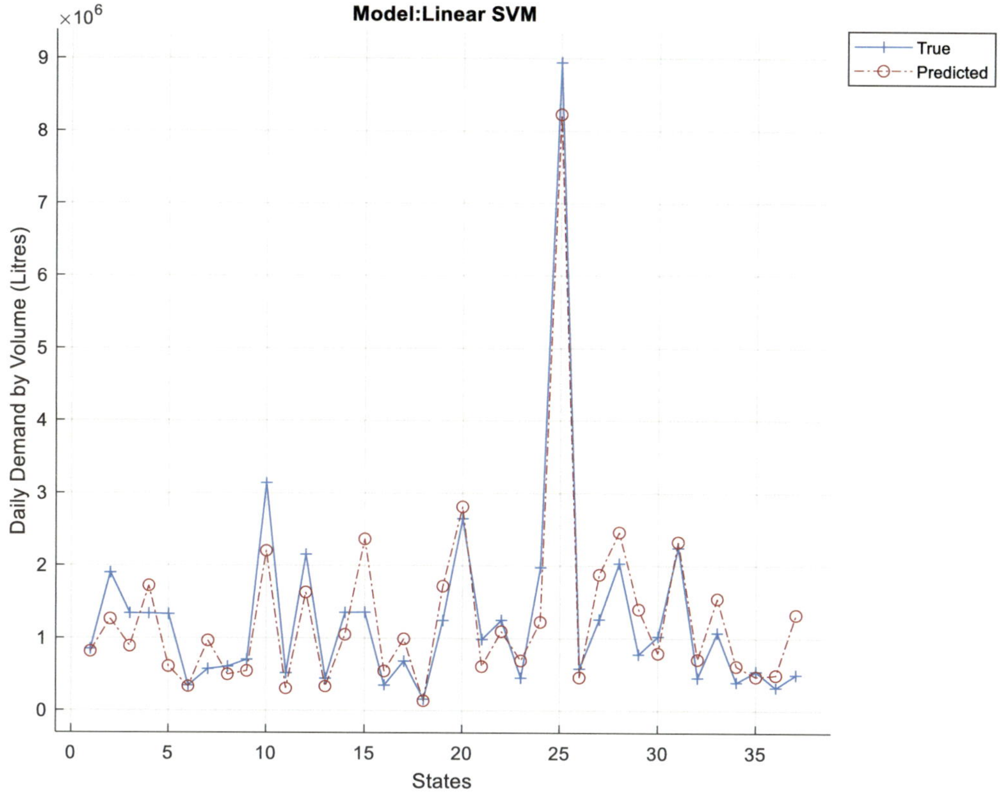

Figure 8.
SVM: States vs. volume demand.

vi. Energy efficiency, carbon intensity, and spill and pollution volume and frequency

Accurate forecasts from ANN and SVM optimize production, transportation, and inventory, reducing waste, energy use, and emissions. These models indirectly enhance sustainability by minimizing adjustments in operations, unlike LR and DT.

vii. Forecast accuracy and technology adoption

ANN and SVM outperform LR and DT in forecast accuracy, with lower variance in high-demand areas. **Table 5** shows ANN (28kb, 2.009s training) and SVM (40kb, 5.4843s training) excel in speed and size, offering technological advantages for deployment.

viii. Risk management and long-term strategy

ANN and SVMs' accurate forecasts improve risk management across operations, enabling better emergency planning, maintenance, and resource allocation. They support long-term strategies such as electric trucks and renewable energy integration, enhancing efficiency and sustainability.

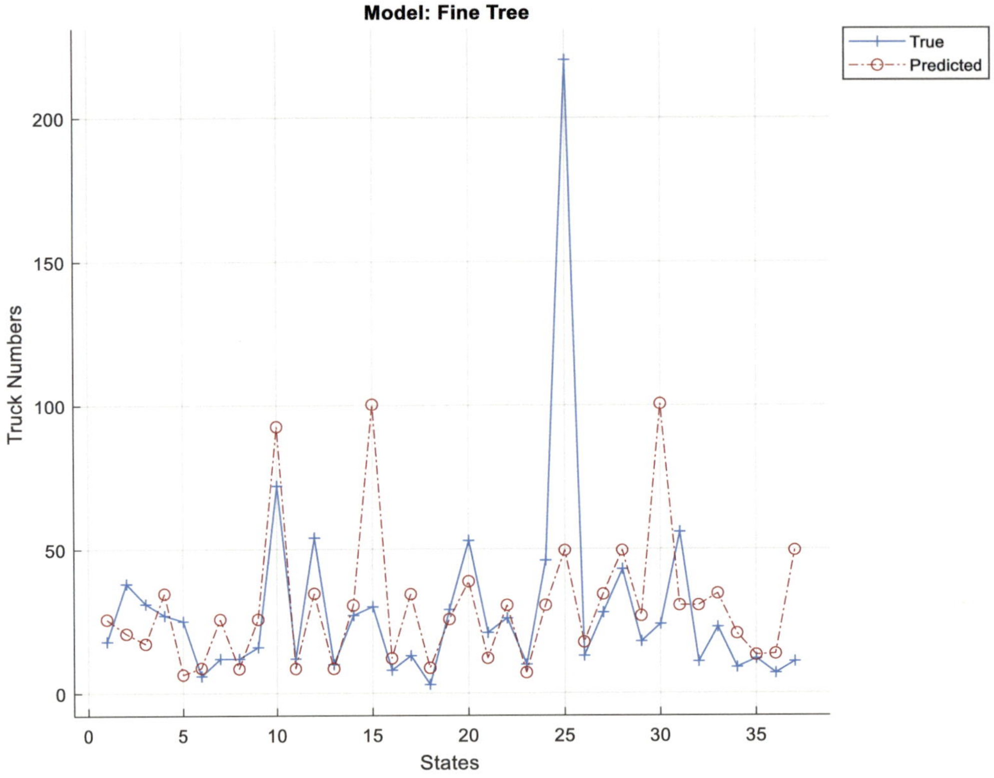

Figure 9.
DT: States vs. demand trucks.

7.5 Applications to the Nigerian petroleum industry

The Nigerian petroleum industry, a critical economic driver, involves stakeholders such as regulatory authorities, refinery operators, oil marketers, logistics companies, investors, and local communities. ML models, particularly ANN and SVMs, provide accurate demand forecasting, enabling stakeholders to optimize operations, reduce costs, and enhance economic stability. This document outlines the applications, benefits, challenges, and performance of ML models in the downstream petroleum sector, focusing on refining, distribution, and logistics.

ML-based demand forecasting supports various stakeholders in Nigeria's petroleum industry:

- NNPC: Through its subsidiary, Pipelines and Products Marketing Company (PPMC), NNPC uses demand predictions to plan imports, manage refinery outputs, and maintain depot stock levels. This reduces fuel scarcity, minimizes emergency import costs, and coordinates with Dangote Refinery for domestic supply.

- The NMDPRA: Accurate forecasts help regulate fuel pricing, ensure quality compliance, and guide infrastructure investments in pipelines, storage, and refinery upgrades.

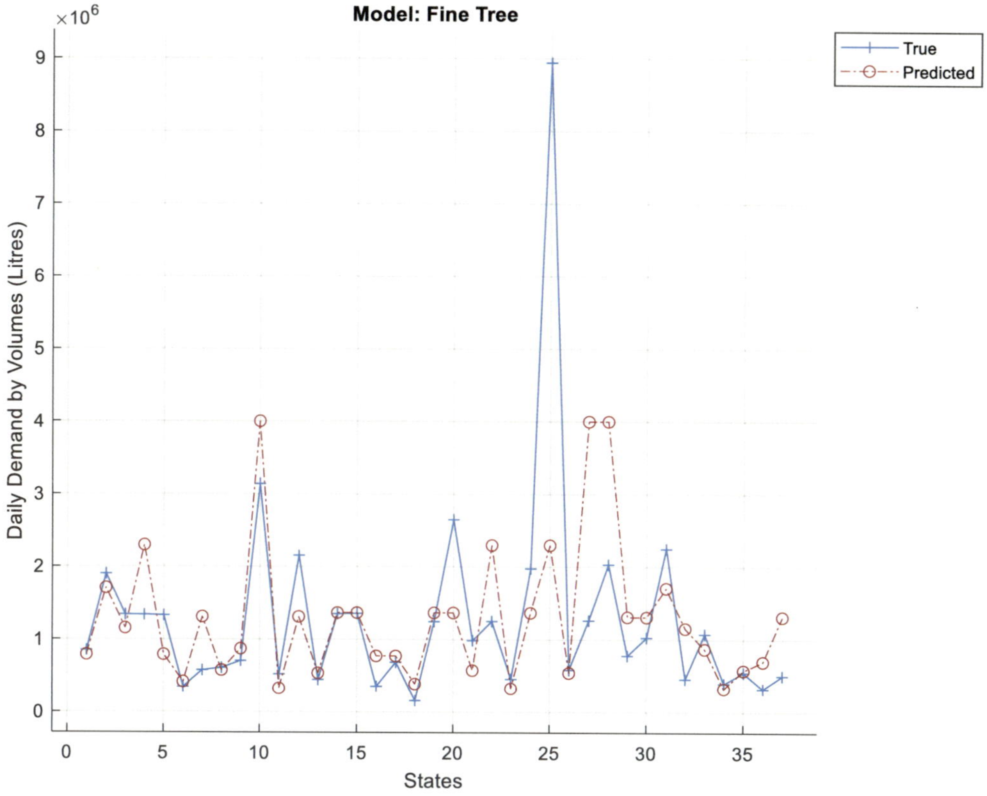

Figure 10.
DT: States vs. demand volume.

- Refineries: Dangote Refinery, state-owned refineries (e.g., Port Harcourt, Warri, Kaduna), and modular refineries adjust production schedules, optimize crude oil intake, and prioritize product mixes (e.g., PMS during festive travel peaks).

- Oil marketers: Major marketers (e.g., TotalEnergies, Mobil, Oando) and the Independent Petroleum Marketers Association of Nigeria (IPMAN) optimize import schedules, storage, and distribution networks, reducing overstocking (capital tie-up) and understocking (lost sales).

- Logistics and transportation companies: These firms optimize fleet sizes, delivery schedules, and routes (e.g., selecting refineries or alternative paths), minimizing idle time, fuel wastage, and transportation costs. Regional demand forecasts enable state-specific resource allocation.

- Investors and financial institutions: Demand forecasts provide market visibility, encouraging investments in refineries and infrastructure. Banks gain confidence in financing projects with assured demand.

- Local communities: In oil-producing regions, accurate forecasting supports community development trust funds, reducing operational disruptions by ensuring fair resource allocation.

ML modelsKPIs	Linear regression	ANN	Decision tree	Support vector machine
Inventory management	3	5	3	5
Production planning	3	5	3	5
Procurement	3	5	3	5
Supplier relationship	3	4	2	5
Risk management	3	5	3	4
Financial planning	4	4	3	5
Long term strategy	4	5	4	5
Technology	4	5	4	5
Lead time sensitivity	4	5	4	5
Localized decision-making	3	4	3	5
Marketing and sales	3	4	3	5
Dynamics adjustment	3	4	3	5
Transportation	4	5	4	4
Pipeline utilization	3	5	3	4
Refinery utilization	4	4	4	5
Customer satisfaction	3	5	2	5
Forecasting accuracy	3	5	3	5
Carbon intensity	3	4	3	4
Energy efficiency	4	4	4	4
Spill/pollution volume and frequency	5	5	5	5
Total	69	92	66	91

1 = very weak, 2 = weak, 3 = average, 4 = strong, 5 = very strong.

Table 4.
KPIs for ML models.

	Linear regression	ANN	Simple vector machine	Decision tree
Prediction speed	500s	1,300s	690s	930s
Training time	3.808s	2.009s	5.4843s	3.1737s
Model size	261kb	28kb	40kb	15kb

Table 5.
The prediction speed, training time, and model size.

- Petrochemical and fertilizer industries: These allied downstream sectors benefit from demand forecasts to plan production and raw material procurement, thereby enhancing supply chain efficiency.

ML models enhance efficiency across the petroleum supply chain through inventory management; accurate demand forecasts prevent overstocking (reducing inventory costs) and understocking (avoiding lost sales), addressing issues such as deadstock from imported products. Production optimization is achieved by adjusting refinery output to meet demand, for example, increasing gasoline production during high-demand periods. Then, through logistics and distribution, optimized fleet and route planning reduce transportation costs and improve delivery efficiency. It is also applied to risk mitigation through forecasting, which mitigates product shortages, stabilizes allied industries (e.g., petrochemicals), and reduces economic ripple effects. These collective benefits promote good policy and attract investment by providing reliable demand data that informs government policies and attracts private sector investments in infrastructure. For example, ANN models capture nonlinear demand patterns, improving forecast accuracy for volatile markets.

Meanwhile, inaccurate ML predictions lead to significant challenges, such as overprediction resulting in excess inventory, wasted resources, poor investment decisions, and operational inefficiencies that increase costs. In contrast, underprediction also leads to resource shortages, delayed deliveries, customer dissatisfaction, lost sales opportunities, and higher maintenance costs due to suboptimal operations. However, model maintenance, in the form of regular retraining, is needed to adapt to changing market dynamics, requiring computational resources and expertise. To address these, optimized ML models (e.g., combined ANN and SVM) balance accuracy and efficiency, minimizing errors and supporting economic stability.

A study comparing ML models for petroleum demand forecasting in Nigeria evaluated their performance against supply chain KPIs. The results are summarized in **Table 6**.

ANN and SVM outperformed traditional models such as ARIMA, offering faster execution (seconds vs. minutes) and lower costs due to reduced manpower. Their ability to handle large datasets efficiently makes them suitable for personal computers, even with increased data volumes. ANN excels in capturing nonlinear demand patterns, while SVM handles high-dimensional data effectively.

The study recommends combining ANN and SVM for demand forecasting in Nigeria's petroleum industry due to their high accuracy, fast execution, and cost-effectiveness. These models enable stakeholders to:

- Plan production, inventory, and logistics efficiently.
- Attract investors by highlighting regional demand trends for industrial development.
- Support infrastructure investments and policy formulation.
- Regularly update models with new data to maintain accuracy in dynamic markets.

ML models, particularly ANN and SVM, transform Nigeria's petroleum industry by providing accurate demand forecasts. These enable stakeholders to optimize

Model	Performance rating (over 20 KPIs)	Execution time
ANN	High (outperforms ARIMA)	Seconds
SVM	High (comparable to ANN)	Seconds
ARIMA (traditional)	Moderate	Minutes (costly, labor-intensive)

Table 6.
Performance of ML models for petroleum demand forecasting.

operations, reduce costs, mitigate risks, and drive economic growth. By addressing forecasting challenges and leveraging high-performing models, the industry can achieve operational efficiency and attract investment for sustainable development.

8. Conclusion

This study evaluates four ML models, selected based on their performances. We trained and tested a 92-day dataset using ML models to predict PMS demand in Nigeria. ANN and SVM emerged at the top of the performance ranking with RMSE values of 0.1425 and 3.5252 on test data, respectively, outperforming LR (27.337) and DT (23.088). The top-performing models have highlighted their ability to predict nonlinear demand patterns, reducing RMSE by 20–25% when benchmarked against LR. The proposed combined usage of ANN and SVM in the Nigerian petroleum industry would leverage their complementary abilities. ANN can recognize demand patterns, and SVM's geometric precision enables robust prediction, which is further validated when measured against KPIs in **Table 4**.

Policymakers, refinery owners and operators, transportation companies, and other stakeholders in the industry can adopt these models for actionable insights and practical deployments. For example, the NNPC can track PMS consumption and identify the areas where fluctuations occur compared to the 26.5% quarterly drop without a justifiable explanation. NNPC's subsidiary, PPMC, can use accurate predictions to mitigate fuel scarcity and avoid up to 15% emergency importation costs based on historical overstocking data. The same can be used for optimal collaboration with Dangote Refinery's 650,000 bpd output for domestic and export needs. This helps to foster relationships among the actors and build resilience in the supply chain of the industry, which translates into a stable economy. NMDPRA, as a regulator, can monitor trends in demand and regions to align proposals for infrastructure upgrades, such as pipeline capacities. MOMAN and IPMAN can reduce their deadstock losses (6% of PMS inventory) by matching demand and purchases. LR's 180% truck overestimation is a minimizable risk, leading to enhanced cost efficiency and customer satisfaction if accurate demand prediction is applied.

Despite being limited to only PMS and a 92-day dataset, our work bridges the knowledge gap in Nigerian data-driven SCM within the downstream petroleum industry. Our findings outperformed traditional statistical methods such as ARIMA, with a reported 30% higher RMSE in a similar context. This chapter lays a solid foundation for resilient, AI-driven petroleum SCM in emerging economies. The results obtained have direct impacts on downstream refineries' production planning and the effective distribution of products. Our next chapter presents two different but connected works on strategies for petroleum product production and improved distribution strategies for petroleum products in Nigeria.

Acknowledgments

Special appreciation goes to the Petroleum Technology Development Fund (PTDF), Nigeria, for the grants. The support has made every progress achieved so far during this program possible. Thank you.

Author details

Olanrewaju I. Adenekan[1*], Aime Nyoungue[1] and Sophie Hennequin[2]

1 Computer Engineering, Production and Maintenance Laboratory, University of Lorraine, Metz, France

2 Design, Manufacturing and Control Laboratory, University of Lorraine, Metz, France

*Address all correspondence to: olanrewaju-isaac.adenekan@univ-lorraine.fr

IntechOpen

© 2025 The Author(s). Licensee IntechOpen. This chapter is distributed under the terms of the Creative Commons Attribution License (http://creativecommons.org/licenses/by/4.0/), which permits unrestricted use, distribution, and reproduction in any medium, provided the original work is properly cited. (cc) BY

References

[1] Azadeh SS, Aydin N. Data-driven optimization for transport and logistics systems. EURO Journal on Transportation and Logistics. 2023;**12**:100119. DOI: 10.1016/j.ejtl.2023.100119

[2] Pereira MM, Frazzon EM. A data-driven approach to adaptive synchronization of demand and supply in omni-channel retail supply chains. International Journal of Information Management. 2021;**57**:102165. DOI: 10.1016/j.ijinfomgt.2020.102165

[3] Ni D, Xiao Z, Lim MK. A systematic review of the research trends of machine learning in supply chain management. International Journal of Machine Learning and Cybernetics. 2020;**11**(7):1463–1482. DOI: 10.1007/s13042-019-01050-0

[4] Akbari M, Do TNA. A systematic review of machine learning in logistics and supply chain management: Current trends and future directions. Benchmarking: An International Journal. 2021;**28**(10):2977–3005. DOI: 10.1108/BIJ-10-2020-0514

[5] Tirkolaee EB, Sadeghi S, Mooseloo FM, Vandchali HR, Aeini S. Application of machine learning in supply chain management: A comprehensive overview of the main areas. Mathematical Problems in Engineering. 2021;**2021**:e1476043. DOI: 10.1155/2021/1476043

[6] Kuang L, *et al.* Application and development trend of artificial intelligence in petroleum exploration and development. Petroleum Exploration and Development. 2021;**48**(1):1–14. DOI: 10.1016/S1876-3804(21)60001-0

[7] Mirza MA, Ghoroori M, Chen Z. Intelligent petroleum engineering. Engineering. 2022;**18**:27–32. DOI: 10.1016/j.eng.2022.06.009

[8] Haoudi Y, Yazdani MA, Roy D, Hennequin S. Demand prediction based on machine learning algorithms for optimal distribution of insulin. IFAC-PapersOnLine. 2023;**56**(2): 10174–10179. DOI: 10.1016/j.ifacol.2023.10.893

[9] Liu Y, Yan G, Settanni A. Forecasting the transportation energy demand with the help of optimization artificial neural network using an improved red fox optimizer (IRFO). Heliyon. 2023;**9**(11): e21599. DOI: 10.1016/j.heliyon.2023.e21599

[10] Horal Liliana, Khvostina, Inesa, Reznik, Nadiia *et al* RWTH Aachen University. Predicting the Economic Efficiency of the Business Model of an Industrial Enterprise Using Machine Learning Methods. In: Kiv, Arnold. CEUR-Workshop July 13-18, 2020; **2713**. Odessa, Ukraine;334–351. DOI: 10.31812/123456789/4476. [Accessed: 2020-October-26]

[11] Kantasa-ard A, Nouiri M, Bekrar A, Ait El Cadi A, Sallez Y. Machine learning for demand forecasting in the physical internet: A case study of agricultural products in Thailand. International Journal of Production Research. 2021;**59**(24):7491–7515. DOI: 10.1080/00207543.2020.1844332

[12] Islam S, Amin SH, Wardley LJ. Machine learning and optimization models for supplier selection and order

allocation planning. International Journal of Production Economics. 2021;**242**:108315. DOI: 10.1016/j.ijpe.2021.108315

[13] Lee C-Y, Chou B-J, Huang C-F. Data science and reinforcement learning for price forecasting and raw material procurement in petrochemical industry. Advanced Engineering Informatics. 2022;**51**:101443. DOI: 10.1016/j.aei.2021.101443

[14] Bousqaoui H, Slimani I, Achchab S. Comparative analysis of short-term demand predicting models using ARIMA and deep learning. International Journal of Electrical and Computer Engineering (IJECE). 2021;**11**(4):3319. DOI: 10.11591/ijece.v11i4.pp3319-3328

[15] Salais-Fierro TE, Saucedo-Martinez JA, Rodriguez-Aguilar R, Vela-Haro JM. Demand prediction using a soft-computing approach: A case study of automotive industry. Applied Sciences. 2020;**10**(3):3. DOI: 10.3390/app10030829

[16] Sharma V, Cali Ü, Sardana B, Kuzlu M, Banga D, Pipattanasomporn M. Data-driven short-term natural gas demand forecasting with machine learning techniques. Journal of Petroleum Science & Engineering. 2021;**206**:108979. DOI: 10.1016/j.petrol.2021.108979

[17] Wang Q, *et al.* A novel method for petroleum and natural gas resource potential evaluation and prediction by support vector machines (SVM). Applied Energy. 2023;**351**:121836. DOI: 10.1016/j.apenergy.2023.121836

[18] Al-Rbeawi S. A review of modern approaches of digitalization in oil and gas industry. Upstream Oil and Gas Technology. 2023;**11**:100098. DOI: 10.1016/j.upstre.2023.100098

[19] Tsilingeridis O, Moustaka V, Vakali A. Design and development of a forecasting tool for the identification of new target markets by open time-series data and deep learning methods. Applied Soft Computing. 2023;**132**:109843. DOI: 10.1016/j.asoc.2022.109843

[20] Khan A, *et al.* Forecasting electricity consumption based on machine learning to improve performance: A case study for the organization of petroleum exporting countries (OPEC). Computers and Electrical Engineering. 2020;**86**:106737. DOI: 10.1016/j.compeleceng.2020.106737

[21] Kapoor G, Wichitaksorn N. Electricity price forecasting in New Zealand: A comparative analysis of statistical and machine learning models with feature selection. Applied Energy. 2023;**347**:121446. DOI: 10.1016/j.apenergy.2023.121446

[22] Cheraghi Y, Kord S, Mashayekhizadeh V. Application of machine learning techniques for selecting the most suitable enhanced oil recovery method; challenges and opportunities. Journal of Petroleum Science & Engineering. 2021;**205**:108761. DOI: 10.1016/j.petrol.2021.108761

[23] Hussain M, Zhang T, Seema M. Adoption of big data analytics for energy pipeline condition assessment - A systematic review. International Journal of Pressure Vessels and Piping. 2023;**206**:105061. DOI: 10.1016/j.ijpvp.2023.105061

[24] Rachman A, Zhang T, Ratnayake RMC. Applications of

machine learning in pipeline integrity management: A state-of-the-art review. International Journal of Pressure Vessels and Piping. 2021;**193**:104471. DOI: 10.1016/j.ijpvp.2021.104471

[25] Momenitabar M, Dehdari Ebrahimi Z, Ghasemi P. Designing a sustainable bioethanol supply chain network: A combination of machine learning and meta-heuristic algorithms. Industrial Crops and Products. 2022;**189**:115848. DOI: 10.1016/j.indcrop.2022.115848

[26] Filom S, Amiri AM, Razavi S. Applications of machine learning methods in port operations – A systematic literature review. Transportation Research Part E Logistics & Transportation Review. 2022;**161**:102722. DOI: 10.1016/j.tre.2022.102722

[27] Odupitan E, 'Effects of Crashing Crude Oil Prices on Oil Producing Countries', p. 41

[28] Cho HU, *et al.* Comparative analysis of the optimized ANN, SVM, and tree ensemble models using Bayesian optimization for predicting GSHP COP. Journal of Building Engineering. 2021;**44**:103411. DOI: 10.1016/j.jobe.2021.103411

[29] Riahi Y, Saikouk T, Gunasekaran A, Badraoui I. Artificial intelligence applications in supply chain: A descriptive bibliometric analysis and future research directions. Expert Systems with Applications. 2021;**173**:114702. DOI: 10.1016/j.eswa.2021.114702

[30] Velidandi A, *et al.* State-of-the-art and future directions of machine learning for biomass characterization and for sustainable biorefinery. Journal of Energy Chemistry. 2023;**81**:42–63

[31] Hribar R, Potočnik P, Šilc J, Papa G. A comparison of models for forecasting the residential natural gas demand of an urban area. Energy. 2019;**167**:511–522. DOI: 10.1016/j.energy.2018.10.175

[32] Sircar A, Yadav K, Rayavarapu K, Bist N, Oza H. Application of machine learning and artificial intelligence in oil and gas industry. Petroleum Research. 2021;**6**(4):379–391. DOI: 10.1016/j.ptlrs.2021.05.009

[33] Kılıç Depren S, Kartal MT, Çoban Çelikdemir N, Depren Ö. Energy consumption and environmental degradation nexus: A systematic review and meta-analysis of fossil fuel and renewable energy consumption. Ecological Informatics. 2022;**70**:101747. DOI: 10.1016/j.ecoinf.2022.101747

[34] Sadeqi-Arani Z, Kadkhodaie A. A bibliometric analysis of the application of machine learning methods in the petroleum industry. Results in Engineering. 2023;**20**:101518. DOI: 10.1016/j.rineng.2023.101518

[35] Zhou D, *et al.* Dynamic simulation of natural gas pipeline network based on interpretable machine learning model. Energy. 2022;**253**:124068. DOI: 10.1016/j.energy.2022.124068

[36] Araujo GS, Gaglianone WP. Machine learning methods for inflation forecasting in Brazil: New contenders versus classical models. Latin American Journal of Central Banking. 2023;**4**(2):100087. DOI: 10.1016/j.latcb.2023.100087

[37] Lu H, Iseley T, Matthews J, Liao W, Azimi M. An ensemble model based on

relevance vector machine and multi-objective Salp swarm algorithm for predicting burst pressure of corroded pipelines. Journal of Petroleum Science & Engineering. 2021;**203**:108585. DOI: 10.1016/j.petrol.2021.108585

[38] Yang Z, *et al.* A graph neural network (GNN) method for assigning gas calorific values to natural gas pipeline networks. Energy. 2023;**278**:127875. DOI: 10.1016/j.energy.2023.127875

[39] Das K, Kumar R, Krishna A. Analyzing electric vehicle battery health performance using supervised machine learning. Renewable and Sustainable Energy Reviews. 2024;**189**:113967. DOI: 10.1016/j.rser.2023.113967

Chapter 5

An Investigation of Keyword Extraction in Arabic and Turkish Employing BERT Models

Bilal Babayigit and Hamza Sattuf

Abstract

Keyword extraction is a fundamental task in natural language processing (NLP), playing a crucial role in information retrieval, document summarization, indexing, and content categorization. Its importance is especially evident in academic research, where high-quality keywords are essential for accurately representing the core content of scholarly articles and enabling efficient discovery. While keyword extraction has seen substantial progress across many languages, both Arabic and Turkish continue to pose unique challenges due to their complex linguistic structures. Turkish, with its agglutinative morphology and intricate syntactic patterns, presents difficulties for standard extraction methods, as words often contain multiple suffixes that encode grammatical and semantic relationships. Likewise, Arabic features nonlinear word formation, rich morphology, and limited availability of annotated corpora, which further complicate keyword identification. These challenges necessitate the adoption of advanced strategies that extend beyond traditional rule-based or statistical techniques. This chapter proposal outlines a comprehensive review of recent research focused on keyword extraction for Arabic and Turkish texts, particularly those that employ deep learning techniques based on Bidirectional Encoder Representations from Transformers (BERT). This chapter surveys state-of-the-art methodologies, evaluating how modern BERT-based models are adapted for morphologically rich languages. It also discusses the integration of classical NLP components with transformer-based models to improve performance. By analyzing and synthesizing findings from the latest published studies, this chapter aims to highlight effective approaches, identify current limitations, and propose best practices for keyword extraction in Arabic and Turkish. The ultimate goal is to support further development in NLP, especially in low-resource and complex languages.

Keywords: keyword extraction, natural language processing (NLP), Turkish, Arabic, BERT (Bidirectional Encoder Representations from Transformers) model, deep learning

1. Introduction

Keyword extraction has become an essential task in the field of natural language processing (NLP), utilized on various digital platforms every day. The growth in digital textual data has led to the need for systems to efficiently identify, index, summarize, and retrieve valuable information. Accurate extraction of keywords and key-phrases is very important for tasks such as automatic indexing, content recommendation, document clustering, and semantic search engines. The explosive growth of digital text is driving a stronger need for advanced, language-agnostic keyword extraction.

Traditionally, the keyword extraction task has been addressed using unsupervised statistical and graph-based methods such as Term Frequency–Inverse Document Frequency (TF-IDF) [1] and TextRank [2]. These methods fundamentally rely on statistical heuristics that treat words as independent tokens, ignoring the deeper syntactic and semantic relations that shape meaning in natural language. Such simplifications are especially limiting when dealing with languages whose linguistic structures differ significantly from English. Although significant progress has been made in high-resource languages such as English, Chinese, and German, morphologically rich and low-resource languages such as Turkish and Arabic remain underexplored [3].

1.1 Challenges in Turkish and Arabic keyword extraction

Turkish and Arabic are two major languages that stand out globally for their importance and complex linguistic structures. With over 80 million native speakers worldwide, Turkish is notable for its ability to generate new words by adding multiple suffixes to base words, resulting in a vast and complex vocabulary that poses difficulties for tasks such as word segmentation, base form identification, and vocabulary breadth [4]. Arabic, spoken by over 420 million people across more than 25 countries, presents unique challenges due to its root-based, nonlinear word formation process, where roots are inserted into predefined patterns to create words [5]. Both languages present significant linguistic challenges due to their complex structures. Turkish employs agglutination, which allows for the formation of numerous word forms by adding suffixes. In contrast, Arabic uses a root-and-pattern system of morphology, which includes notable differences among dialects [5]. These characteristics make tasks such as tokenization and semantic clarification more challenging. Traditional keyword extraction methods struggle to fully capture the diversity and complexity found in texts written in Turkish and Arabic due to these distinctive morphological characteristics.

1.2 The rise of BERT in keyword extraction

Over the past five years, deep learning models have reshaped NLP. Chief among these is Bidirectional Encoder Representations from Transformers (BERT), introduced by Google [6], which has become a foundational model for language understanding tasks. By capturing context from both the left and right simultaneously, BERT models can understand the meaning of words in context, making them well suited for morphologically rich languages such as Turkish and Arabic. After the success of the original English version of BERT,

DOI: http://dx.doi.org/10.5772/intechopen.1012609

researchers developed multilingual BERT (mBERT) along with language-specific variants to better address the unique characteristics of non-English languages. Modified versions of BERT, such as AraBERT [7] for Arabic and BERTurk [8] for Turkish, have demonstrated notable benefits for language processing in these languages. However, the use of BERT-based models for keyword extraction in these languages remains largely unexamined and lacks a comprehensive study. While BERT and its various versions have significantly advanced tasks in NLP, such as sentiment analysis and question answering, their application in keyword extraction – particularly in languages other than English – remains an area of ongoing research and development.

1.3 Motivation and scope

This chapter offers a detailed analysis of BERT-based keyword extraction for Turkish and Arabic and examines the associated challenges and opportunities. It surveys methodological approaches in the literature, analyzes the datasets used, evaluates the metrics employed, and highlights language-specific challenges. Despite the advances brought by BERT and similar transformer models, comprehensive reviews focusing specifically on Turkish and Arabic keyword extraction remain limited. To address this gap, this chapter provides the following:

- An exploration of the linguistic challenges unique to Turkish and Arabic.
- A review of the evolution of keyword extraction methods, with a focus on BERT-based approaches.
- Comparative analyses of model performance, datasets used, and evaluation metrics.

2. Morphological complexity of Turkish and Arabic

Keyword extraction accuracy depends heavily on how well a system handles morphology, especially in languages such as Turkish and Arabic, where single words can represent entire phrases or have multiple meanings. This section provides a brief overview of the main morphological and syntactic features of Turkish and Arabic that are crucial for understanding the challenges in BERT-based keyword extraction for these languages.

2.1 Morphological features of Turkish

Turkish is an agglutinative language, forming words by adding multiple suffixes to a root, each carrying a specific grammatical function [9]. Vowel harmony and consonant alternations shape suffix forms, increasing morphological complexity. This leads to a high number of surface word forms, causing data sparsity and ambiguity in NLP tasks. As shown in **Table 1**, a single Turkish word can express the meaning of an entire phrase in English. Standard tokenizers often struggle with morphologically rich languages such as Turkish, where words are formed by adding multiple suffixes to a root. These tokenizers typically treat the entire word as a single

Word	Meaning	Breakdown
Kitapçıdaymış	Apparently, (he/she) was at the bookstore.	kitap (book) + çı (seller/person) + da (at) + imiş (apparently)
Göremeyeceğim	I will not be able to see.	gör (see) + e (ability) + me (not) + y (buffer letter) + ecek (future) + im (I)
Geliyorum	I am coming.	gel (come) + iyor (ing) + um (I)

Table 1.
Turkish agglutination examples.

unit, failing to split it into its meaningful components. Tools such as Zemberek [10] help split morphemes before BERT encodes them, as shown in **Table 2**.

2.2 Morphological features of Arabic

Arabic is a morphologically rich and highly inflectional language, characterized by its root-and-pattern system. Most words are derived from triliteral consonantal roots, which carry the core semantic meaning. Vowel patterns, prefixes, suffixes, and infixes are then applied to these roots to create different word forms, expressing tense, voice, number, gender, and case [11]. This nonlinear morphology allows for extensive word variation, where a single root can generate dozens of related words, as shown in **Table 3**. This richness poses significant challenges for tokenization and NLP tasks.

Tools such as the Qalsadi lemmatizer [12] normalize words to their original roots through morphological analysis, converting tokens into their canonical dictionary forms, or lemmas. Qalsadi, an Arabic morphological analyzer built on the Tashaphyne stemmer, integrates the PyArabic library to enable efficient processing of alphabetical characters and diacritics. Its core functions include removing tashkeel (diacritical marks), handling shadda (gemination), and addressing inflectional variations by removing the final diacritic when necessary. By breaking Arabic words down into their constituent morphemes, Qalsadi improves the accuracy of linguistic analysis. An example of the lemmatization process is shown in **Table 4**.

2.3 Syntactic properties of Turkish and Arabic

Turkish follows a Subject–Verb–Object (SVO) order, while Arabic typically uses Verb–Subject–Object (VSO) in formal registers, though SVO appears in colloquial speech. In Turkish, verbs agree with the subject in person and number only. In Arabic, verbs agree with the subject in person, number, and gender, with agreement patterns differing between VSO and SVO structures.

Word	Evlerimizdenmişsiniz
Without Zemberek	[UNK]
With Zemberek	ev + ler + imiz + den + miş + siniz

Table 2.
Zemberek tools example.

Root	Word	Pattern	Meaning
كتب	kitab	كتاب	Book
كتب	maktab	مكتب	Office
كتب	maktub	مكتوب	Written
كتب	katib	كاتب	Writer

Table 3.
Arabic root-pattern morphology.

Original sentence	Lemmatized sentence using Qalsadi
الصديقان يلعبان في الملعب	صديق يلعب ملعب

Table 4.
Qalsadi example.

3. Keyword extraction techniques – from traditional to deep learning

This section outlines the evolution of keyword extraction methods, from early statistical techniques to advanced transformer-based approaches, highlighting the shift from rule-based and statistical models to machine learning and deep learning. It emphasizes the impact of these developments on Turkish and Arabic languages and sets the stage for understanding modern BERT-based KE technologies.

Keyword extraction can be categorized into two types: supervised and unsupervised methods. Each approach employs various algorithms and techniques to effectively extract keywords.

- **Unsupervised keyword extraction:** Traditionally, keyword extraction has primarily been explored through unsupervised methods. Unsupervised keyword extraction does not require labeled data. Instead, it uses statistical, linguistic, or graph-based methods to determine the importance of words and phrases based on their distribution in the text, among other features [13].

- **TF-IDF:** TF-IDF [14, 15] is a statistical measure that evaluates how relevant a word is to a document in a collection of documents. It increases proportionally with the frequency of the tokens in a document. TF-IDF requires a large corpus to improve its performance.

- **KP-Miner:** KP-Miner [16] is another unsupervised method that uses not only statistical frequency but also some other features such as word length, minimum occurrence, and positional information to extract key-phrases. These additional features aim to filter out less significant words.

- **Rapid Automatic Keyword Extraction (RAKE):** RAKE [17] is a fast, simple algorithm that identifies keywords by analyzing the frequency of word appearance and its cooccurrence with other words in the text.

- **YAKE:** YAKE [18] is a lightweight, unsupervised, automatic keyword extraction algorithm that emphasizes single-document keyword extraction. It calculates a keyword score using term frequency and some hand-crafted features such as word position, word frequency, and context to rank keywords.

- **TextRank:** TextRank [19, 20] is a graph-based ranking model for text processing, inspired by Google's PageRank algorithm. TextRank builds an undirected, unweighted graph from the text, where nodes are words or phrases and edges are based on their cooccurrence relations. The importance of each node (word or phrase) is then scored based on its connectivity.

- **SGRank:** SGRank [21] is an improved version of TextRank. SGRank focuses on statistical and graph-based scoring to identify terms that not only appear frequently together but also have strong relevance to the overall context of the document.

These unsupervised methods benefit from requiring minimal data and offering faster inference; however, their accuracy tends to be lower because they extract keywords without a deep semantic understanding of the document.

- **Supervised keyword extraction:** Supervised keyword extraction relies on labeled datasets to train models that can learn to identify keywords based on features derived from the text. These models require a training phase, where they learn the patterns associated with keywords from a set of prelabeled datasets. Supervised keyword extraction typically results in higher accuracy and relevance compared to unsupervised methods [17]. Supervised keyword extraction can be further categorized into two main strategies: classification-based and generation-based approaches.

- **Classification-based approach:** In a classification-based approach, the task of keyword extraction is treated as a binary classification problem where each candidate word or phrase is classified as either a keyword or not. Luan et al. [22] identified keywords by utilizing part-of-speech embeddings along with a combination of word and character features. Another classification-based method was proposed by Chun et al. [23], where the authors introduced a new embedding approach for sequence labeling that combines character-level and word-level embeddings to find the most significant character or word in a document.

- **Generation-based approach:** Generation-based approaches treat keyword extraction as a sequence-to-sequence (seq2seq) task, where the aim is to generate a sequence of keywords from a given text. This method often employs advanced neural network architectures, such as recurrent neural networks (RNNs) [24], transformers, or models such as BART [25], which can understand the context and semantics of text more deeply than traditional models.

Figure 1 categorizes automatic keyword extraction methods. Each of these methods has its strengths and weaknesses, and the choice of a particular method can

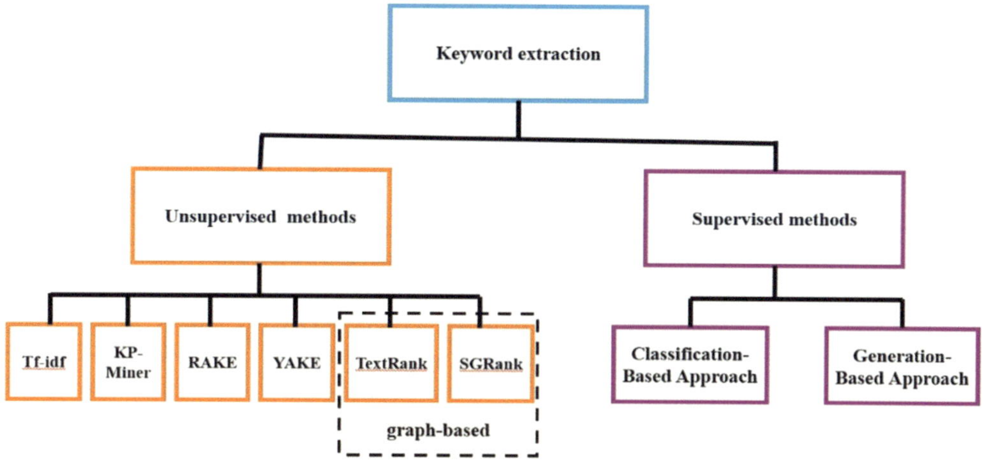

Figure 1.
Categorization of automatic keyword extraction methods.

depend on the specific characteristics of the text corpus, the desired level of accuracy, and the computational resources available. The development of deep learning models such as RNN, BART, and BERT has introduced powerful options for supervised learning, while traditional unsupervised techniques such as TF-IDF and TextRank continue to be effective for scenarios where labeled data are not available. However, traditional methods often struggle with morphologically rich and highly inflectional languages such as Arabic and Turkish, where complex word forms and rich morphology can reduce their effectiveness compared to deep learning approaches.

Traditional keyword extraction methods such as TF–IDF, RAKE, and TextRank are mainly built for languages that have simpler morphological structures. However, in morphologically rich languages such as Turkish and Arabic, these techniques face challenges due to the multitude of word forms created through inflection and derivation. Moreover, standard tokenization and stemming techniques often struggle to accurately segment or normalize complex word forms, leading to important keywords being split, misrepresented, or completely overlooked. Multiword expressions and compound terms are also tricky to identify using frequency-based heuristics. Consequently, traditional keyword extraction methods often miss the truc semantic significance of terms, underscoring the necessity for more sophisticated, context-aware models. In recent years, transformer architectures and pretrained language models such as BERT have truly taken the spotlight. BERT stands out because it creates contextualized representations, which means that the vectors for the same word can change based on the context, unlike static embeddings. For Turkish and Arabic, modern BERT-based models bridge the gap between rich morphological structures and robust keyword extraction, laying the groundwork for future research in low-resource and dialect-rich settings.

4. Bert-based keyword extraction: State-of-the-art methodologies

BERT, introduced by Google [6], represents a paradigm shift in NLP through its novel approach to pretraining deep bidirectional representations. Unlike previous language representation models that process text in a unidirectional manner – either left-to-right or through shallow concatenation of independently trained left-to-right and right-to-left models – BERT employs a bidirectional training methodology that enables the model to condition on both left and right contexts simultaneously across all layers. BERT utilizes transformer-based encoders to understand bidirectional relationships within text, leading to improved keyword and key-phrase identification, especially in languages such as Turkish and Arabic, which have complex morphology and flexible syntax. Recent studies on BERT-based keyword extraction have converged on three primary methods: leveraging embedding similarities, classifying tokens, and utilizing seq2seq generation.

4.1 Embedding-based similarity approaches

Approaches that rely on embeddings for similarity assessment utilize techniques such as KeyBERT [26], which employs BERT embeddings to measure the cosine similarity between potential phrases and the document's representation. These methods typically entail identifying noun phrases or n-grams through POS tagging, then organizing them based on their semantic coherence with the overall text. Different versions of this approach incorporate sentence transformers (such as all-MiniLM, MPNet) or specialized models such as AraBERT and BERTurk to customize the embeddings for specific language contexts.

4.2 Token classification models

Token classification models conceptualize keyword extraction as a sequence labeling problem, systematically applying the Inside-Outside-Beginning (IOB) annotation scheme to identify and delineate keyword boundaries within continuous text. This methodological framework transforms the keyword extraction task into a structured prediction problem, where each token receives a label indicating its relationship to potential keywords. Researchers [27] applied this approach in a BERT-based model for Turkish academic texts, achieving exceptional performance. Utilizing a large-scale, IOB-tagged dataset of academic theses, the model successfully captured the language's morphological and syntactic complexities, attaining an F-score of 97.77%.

4.3 Sequence-to-sequence (seq2seq) generation

A promising approach to keyword extraction treats it as a generative task, where the model is trained to produce a sequence of keywords directly from the input text. This is achieved through architectures that combine BERT-based encoders with decoders, such as BERT2BERT, mBART, and T5. Although this method requires more computational resources and is sensitive to the quality of the training data, it offers the ability to produce semantically relevant keywords that are not necessarily present in the original text, making it particularly useful for cases where key-phrases are rephrased or implied.

The use of BERT-based methods in Turkish and Arabic languages poses significant challenges due to their unique linguistic characteristics, including agglutination, diacritic uncertainty, and flexible word order. To address these challenges, specialized models (such as BERTurk [8] and AraBERT [7]) have been created and tailored to these languages through large-scale native language datasets. These tailored models have demonstrated improved results in keyword extraction tasks compared to more general multilingual or zero-shot models, highlighting the value of language-specific pretraining.

5. Benchmark evaluations for Turkish and Arabic keyword extraction

Evaluating BERT-based keyword extraction requires high-quality annotated datasets and standardized benchmarks. In Turkish and Arabic, recent efforts to develop such resources have begun to overcome long-standing limitations, enabling more reliable comparisons across models and tasks. However, there remains a noticeable gap, as only a few studies have implemented BERT-based approaches for keyword extraction in both languages. In the following sections, we survey and compare recent studies that have employed BERT models for keyword extraction or closely related NLP tasks.

5.1 Benchmark comparisons of BERT-based models for Turkish

This section presents and analyzes the performance of various transformer-based models applied to Turkish NLP tasks, with a focus on keyword extraction, question answering, and summarization. The highest performance was achieved by BERTurk [27] for token classification using the IOB tagging scheme on the Thesis-Based Keyword Corpus, which consists of over 128,000 Turkish theses. The model reported an outstanding F1-score of 97.77%, highlighting its robustness in structured academic keyword extraction tasks. The large dataset and task-specific fine-tuning are likely contributors to this exceptional result.

Ayan et al. [28] sought to determine companies' business domains by clustering keywords extracted from their official websites. To perform keyword extraction from Turkish text, the authors employed a deep-learning-based approach using Sentence-BERT. Their dataset comprised content gathered from the websites of 25 major Turkish companies, from which relevant keywords were identified. The proposed model achieved an F1-score of 39%.

In a separate study on Turkish Question Answering [29], a new dataset was created by merging THQuAD – the Turkish Historic Question Answering Dataset on Islamic History of Science and Ottoman History – with BQuAD, a Biology Question Answering Dataset. Using this combined dataset, BERTurk (Cased, 128k) achieved an F1-score of 80.84%, demonstrating its strong capability in semantic understanding and contextual reasoning tasks.

Aydın and Kantarcı [30] investigated Turkish keyword extraction using deep-learning-based seq2seq models. They evaluated two architectures: a long short-term memory (LSTM)-based Seq2Seq model and a BERT-based Seq2Seq model on a dataset combining the Turkish Tagged Text Corpus with the Text Summarization–Keyword Extraction Dataset. Performance, measured by ROUGE-1 F1, was 38% for the LSTM model and 39.9% for the BERT model, indicating a slight advantage for the transformer-based approach.

A study on Turkish text summarization [31] applied the text-to-text transfer transformer (T5) model to an original dataset collected from online Turkish news sources, focusing on abstractive summarization. The approach achieved an F1-score of 89.13%, indicating its strong effectiveness for Turkish abstractive summarization.

Method/study	Task	Year	Dataset	F1-score
BERTurk (IOB tagging) [27]	Keyword extraction	2025	Thesis-Based Keyword Corpus (128 K theses)	97.77%
Sentence-BERT [28]	Keyword extraction	2021	Websites of 25 large Turkish companies	39.0%
BERTurk (Cased, 128k) [29]	Question answering	2024	Combined dataset (THQuAD & BQuAD)	80.84%
LSTM-based Seq2Seq model [30]	Keyword extraction	2024	Combined Turkish Tagged Text and Summarization Keyword Extraction Dataset	38.0%
BERT-based Seq2Seq [30]	Keyword extraction	2024	Combined Turkish Tagged Text and Summarization Keyword Extraction Dataset	39.9%
T5 [31]	Abstractive summarization	2023	Dataset collected from online Turkish news sources	89.13%

Table 5.
Comparison of recent BERT models used for Turkish keyword extraction.

Table 5 provides a comparative overview of recent studies utilizing BERT and other transformer-based models for Turkish keyword extraction and related NLP tasks. It includes methodological details, performance metrics, and the specific datasets employed.

Figure 2 shows the comparison of the F1-score or accuracy of BERT-based models applied to Turkish NLP tasks. The horizontal bar chart illustrates the reported F1-scores of six models evaluated across various tasks and datasets. The BERTurk (IOB tagging) model, trained on the Thesis-Based Keyword Corpus, achieves the highest performance with an F1-score of 97.77%, demonstrating the effectiveness of token classification for keyword extraction. In contrast, Sentence-BERT applied to corporate websites yields a substantially lower score of 39.0%, indicating weaker suitability for this task. For question answering, BERTurk (Cased, 128k) achieves 80.84%, showing strong but comparatively lower performance than keyword-specific models. Traditional LSTM-based Seq2Seq and BERT-based Seq2Seq architectures perform similarly (38.0% and 39.9%), underperforming compared to more advanced transformer-based methods. Finally, the T5, trained on Turkish news data, demonstrates competitive performance in abstractive summarization with an F1-score of 89.13%. Overall, the results highlight the dominance of domain-specific BERTurk models in Turkish keyword extraction and NLP tasks, while also emphasizing the variation in performance depending on the model architecture and dataset.

5.2 Benchmark comparisons of BERT-based models for Arabic

This section provides a comprehensive review of recent transformer-based approaches applied to Arabic NLP tasks. The surveyed studies cover a range of applications, including term extraction, keyword extraction, and question generation. Their effectiveness is predominantly assessed using the F1-score, which captures the trade-off between precision and recall.

A recent study [32] addressed the challenge of automatic term extraction from domain-specific corpora in Arabic, an area historically dominated by rule-based and statistical approaches due to the lack of annotated resources. The authors

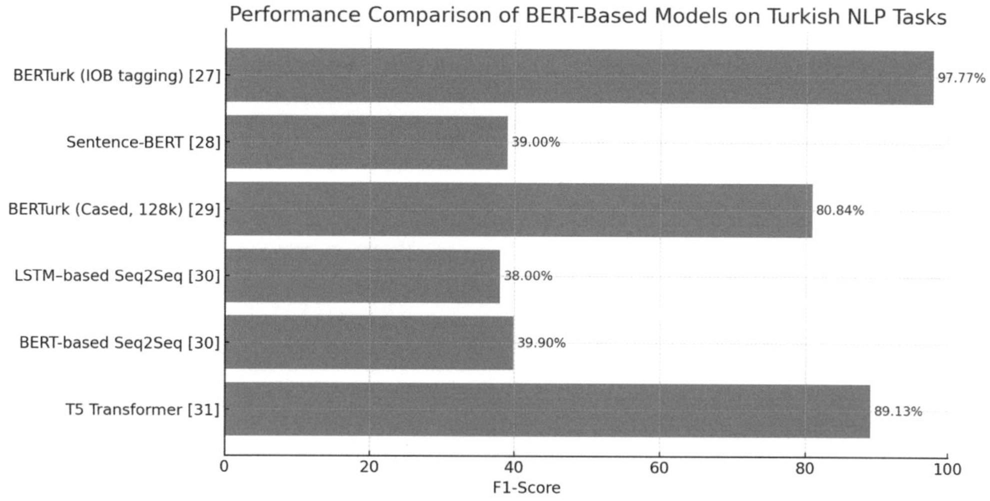

Figure 2.
Performance comparison of BERT-based and transformer-based models on Turkish NLP tasks.

introduced AraATE, the first annotated dataset for Arabic automatic term extraction in the field of Arabic linguistics, containing 4,148 sentences, 155,502 tokens, and 4,362 annotated single- and multiword terms across subfields such as lexicography, semantics, pragmatics, phonetics, and semiotics. Three BERT-based models were fine-tuned on AraATE, with AraBERT-base, CAMeLBERT-MSA, and AraBERT-large achieving comparable F1-scores (82%, 81%, and 81%).

Alharbi and Al-Muhtasab [33] investigated deep learning techniques for Arabic key-phrase extraction by framing it as a sequence classification task. They implemented a Bi-LSTM model to determine whether each token in a sequence belonged to a key-phrase. Word embeddings were derived from pretrained models, including Word2Vec and BERT. In addition, the study explored the effect of integrating linguistic, positional, and statistical features with these embeddings. Their best-performing configuration – BERT embeddings combined with linguistic and positional features – achieved an F1-score of 45% on the ArabicKPE dataset.

Al-Qurishi [34] introduced AraLegal-BERT, a domain-specific pretrained model tailored for Arabic legal texts. The model was trained and evaluated on a dataset of approximately 8,000 legal documents, where the most important keywords were manually extracted. Experimental results showed that AraLegal-BERT achieved strong performance across several natural language understanding tasks, with an F1-score of 92% for keyword extraction, substantially outperforming general-purpose Arabic BERT variants.

In Tami et al. (2024) [35], the authors employed KeyBERT, leveraging BERT-based embeddings for keyword extraction as a key component in an automated question-generation pipeline for Arabic science assessments. Their proposed system follows a three-stage process consisting of keyword and key-phrase extraction, question generation, and subsequent ranking. The framework was designed to address the challenges of automatically generating assessment questions in Arabic. Experimental evaluation demonstrated its effectiveness, achieving a precision of 83.50%, a recall of 78.68%, and an F1-score of 80.95%.

Method/study	Task	Year	Dataset	F1-score
AraBERT-base [32]	Term extraction	2025	AraATE	82.0%
CAMeLBERT-MSA [32]	Term extraction	2025	AraATE	81.0%
AraBERT-large [32]	Term extraction	2025	AraATE	81.0%
Bi-LSTM + BERT [33]	Keyword extraction	2022	ArabicKPE dataset	45.0%
AraLegal-BERT [34]	Keyword extraction – legal domain	2022	8,000 legal documents	92.0%
KeyBERT [35]	Keyword extraction	2024	Manually extracted dataset	80.95%
XLM-RoBERTa [36]	Keyword extraction	2024	Not specified	59.69%

Table 6.
Comparison of recent BERT models used for Arabic keyword extraction.

A recent preprint [36] proposed a transformer-based approach for Arabic keyword extraction, incorporating prompt engineering to guide the model toward generating the desired outputs. The study also explored methods for interpreting the inner workings of transformer models, offering insights into how their outputs can be better controlled. The approach was evaluated by comparing automatically extracted keywords against manually annotated ones, achieving an average precision of 0.69. In addition, experiments with XLM-RoBERTa reported an F1-score of 59.69%.

Table 6 provides a comparative overview of recent studies that utilize BERT models for Arabic keyword extraction and related NLP tasks. It includes methodological details, performance metrics, and the specific datasets employed.

Figure 3 shows the comparison of the F1-scores of BERT-based models applied to Arabic NLP tasks. The horizontal bar chart illustrates the reported performance

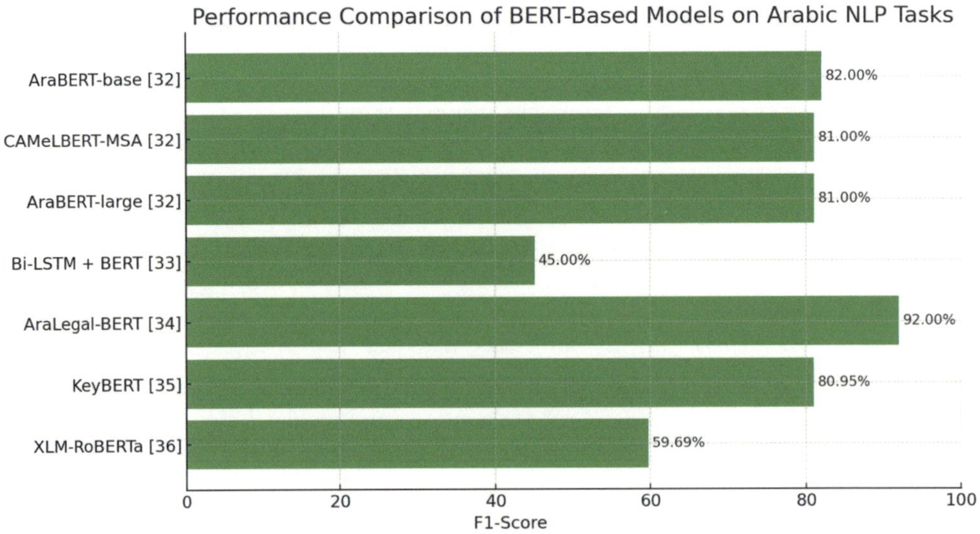

Figure 3.
Performance comparison of BERT-based and transformer-based models on Arabic NLP tasks.

of seven models evaluated across different corpora and applications. AraLegal-BERT, trained on legal texts, achieves the highest score of 92.0%, demonstrating the effectiveness of domain-specific adaptation. General-purpose AraBERT variants perform consistently well, with scores around 81–82%, while KeyBERT also shows strong results at 80.95%. In contrast, XLM-RoBERTa records a lower score of 59.69%, and the Bi-LSTM + BERT hybrid model performs the weakest at 45.0%. Overall, the results highlight the superiority of specialized and domain-adapted models over multilingual and hybrid approaches for Arabic keyword extraction and related tasks.

6. Conclusion

This chapter has provided a systematic exploration of BERT-based keyword extraction in the context of Turkish and Arabic, two morphologically rich and linguistically complex languages. We reviewed the evolution of keyword extraction techniques, examined BERT and its multilingual adaptations, evaluated state-of-the-art methodologies, and discussed language-specific challenges. The analysis highlights that both Turkish and Arabic benefit substantially from BERT-based approaches; however, domain-specific adaptation (e.g., BERTurk for Turkish and AraLegal-BERT for Arabic) consistently leads to superior performance. In contrast, multilingual and generic embeddings underperform compared to specialized monolingual models, underscoring the importance of curated datasets and task-specific fine-tuning for low-resource languages.

Despite these advances, several limitations and challenges remain. The morphological complexity of both languages continues to pose difficulties for tokenization and representation. Resource constraints – particularly the scarcity of large-scale, high-quality annotated corpora – limit broader progress. Furthermore, BERT-based models are inherently large and computationally intensive, restricting their accessibility in low-resource research and deployment settings.

Looking ahead, several research directions emerge as particularly promising. Future work should prioritize developing dialect-aware models capable of handling Arabic regional variations and Turkish colloquial varieties, while exploring cross-lingual transfer learning mechanisms that leverage the morphological similarities between these languages. From a practical standpoint, such advances have immediate applications in digital content management systems, e-commerce platforms, and legal technology solutions, with domain-specific models demonstrating clear commercial viability. However, current limitations, including high computational requirements, domain transfer challenges, and difficulties with code-switching scenarios, highlight the need for more efficient architectures and regular model updates to maintain effectiveness in rapidly evolving linguistic environments. Ultimately, this chapter aims to serve as both a foundational reference and a launch pad for continued innovation in multilingual keyword extraction.

Conflict of interest

The authors declare no conflict of interests.

Author details

Bilal Babayigit[1*] and Hamza Sattuf[2]

1 Department of Computer Engineering, Erciyes University, Kayseri, Türkiye

2 Graduate School of Natural and Applied Sciences, Erciyes University, Kayseri, Türkiye

*Address all correspondence to: bilalb@erciyes.edu.tr

IntechOpen

© 2025 The Author(s). Licensee IntechOpen. This chapter is distributed under the terms of the Creative Commons Attribution License (http://creativecommons.org/licenses/by/4.0/), which permits unrestricted use, distribution, and reproduction in any medium, provided the original work is properly cited.

References

[1] Ramos J Using TF-IDF to determine word relevance in document queries. In: Proceedings of the First Instructional Conference on Machine Learning; 2003. pp. 133–142.

[2] Mihalcea R, Tarau P TextRank: Bringing order into texts. In: Proceedings of the 2004 Conference on Empirical Methods in Natural Language Processing (EMNLP); 2004. pp. 404–411.

[3] Hedderich MA, Lange L, Adel H, Strötgen J, Klakow D A survey on recent approaches for natural language processing in low-resource scenarios. In: Proceedings of the 2021 Conference of the North American Chapter of the Association for Computational Linguistics: Human Language Technologies (NAACL-HLT); 2021. pp. 2545–2568. DOI: 10.18653/v1/2021.naacl-main.201.

[4] Oflazer K, Durgar El-Kahlout I Exploring different representational units in English-to-Turkish statistical machine translation. In: Callison-Burch C, Koehn P, Fordyce CS, Monz C, editors. Proceedings of the Second Workshop on Statistical Machine Translation; 2007 Jun; Prague, Czech Republic. Stroudsburg: Association for Computational Linguistics; 2007. pp. 25–32.

[5] Habash, N. Y. Introduction to Arabic Natural Language Processing. In: G. Hirst Ed. Synthesis Lectures on Human Language Technologies (Vol. 3, No. 1). Morgan & Claypool Publishers; 2010. p. 1–187. DOI: 10.2200/S00277ED1V01Y201008HLT010

[6] Devlin J, Chang MW, Lee K, Toutanova KBERT: Pre-training of deep bidirectional transformers for language understanding. In: Proceedings of the 2019 Conference of the North American Chapter of the Association for Computational Linguistics: Human Language Technologies (NAACL-HLT); 2019 Jun; Minneapolis, USA. Stroudsburg: Association for Computational Linguistics; 2019. vol. **1**, pp. 4171–4186.

[7] Antoun W, Baly F, Hajj H AraBERT: Transformer-based Model for Arabic Language Understanding. In: Al-Khalifa H, Magdy W, Darwish K, Elsayed T, Mubarak H, editors. Proceedings of the 4th Workshop on Open-Source Arabic Corpora and Processing Tools, with a Shared Task on Offensive Language Detection; 2020 May; Marseille, France. European Language Resource Association; 2020. pp. 9–15.

[8] DBMDZ. dbmdz/bert-base-turkish-uncased [Model]. Hugging Face. (n.d.). Avaliable from: https://huggingface.co/dbmdz/bert-base-turkish-uncased [Accessed: 2025-August-11]

[9] Göksel A, and Kerslake C Turkish: A Comprehensive Grammar. Psychology Press; 2005. 580 p. Available from: https://books.google.com.tr/books/about/Turkish.html?id=7fXCKZmee8QC&redir_esc=y [Accessed: 2025-August-11]

[10] Akın AA, Akın MD. Zemberek: An open source NLP framework for Turkic languages. Structure. 2007;**10**:1–5

[11] Boudlal A. Root and pattern morphology revisited: Verb stem bimoraicity and stem based morphology in Moroccan Arabic. Asinag. 2018;**13**:165–190

[12] Zerrouki T Qalsadi: Arabic morphological analyzer and Lemmatizer for Python. Available from: https://pypi.org//project/qalsadi/ [Accessed: 2025-July-27]

[13] Bae YS, Kim KH, Kim HK, Choi SW, Ko T, Seo HH, Lee HY, Jeon H. Keyword extraction algorithm for classifying smoking status from unstructured bilingual electronic health records based on natural language processing. Applied Sciences. 2021;**11**:8812. DOI: 10.3390/app11198812.

[14] Li J, Fan Q, Zhang K. Keyword extraction based on tf/idf for Chinese news document. Wuhan University Journal of Natural Sciences. 2007;**12** (5):917–921. DOI:10.1007/s11859-007-0038-4.

[15] Sparck Jones K. A statistical interpretation of term specificity and its application in retrieval. In: Document Retrieval Systems. GBR: Taylor Graham Publishing; 1988. pp. 132–142

[16] El-Beltagy SR, Rafea A. KP-Miner: A keyphrase extraction system for English and Arabic documents. Information Systems. 2009;**34** (1):132–144. DOI:10.1016/j.is.2008.05.002.

[17] Rose S, Engel D, Cramer N, Cowley W, et al. Automatic keyword extraction from individual documents. In: Miner G, Elder J, Fast A, Hill T, Nisbet R, Delen D, editors. Text Mining: Applications and Theory. Chichester: Wiley;2010. pp. 1–20. DOI: 10.1002/9780470689646.ch1.

[18] Campos R, Mangaravite V, Pasquali A, Jorge A, Nunes C, Jatowt AYAKE. Keyword extraction from single documents using multiple local features. Information Sciences. 2020;**509**:257–289. DOI: 10.1016/j.ins.2019.09.013.

[19] Wang J, Liu J, Wang C. Keyword extraction based on PageRank. In: Proceedings of the 11th Pacific-Asia Conference on Advances in Knowledge Discovery and Data Mining (PAKDD'07); 2007 May; Nanjing, China. Berlin, Heidelberg: Springer-Verlag; 2007. pp. 857–864.

[20] Mihalcea R, Tarau P TextRank: Bringing order into text. In: Lin D, Wu D, editors. Proceedings of the 2004 Conference on Empirical Methods in Natural Language Processing (EMNLP); 2004 Jul; Barcelona, Spain. Stroudsburg: Association for Computational Linguistics; 2004. pp. 404–411.

[21] Danesh S, Sumner T, Martin JH SGRank: Combining statistical and graphical methods to improve the state of the art in unsupervised keyphrase extraction. In: Palmer M, Boleda G, Rosso P, editors. Proceedings of the Fourth Joint Conference on Lexical and Computational Semantics (*SEM 2015); 2015 Jun; Denver, Colorado. Stroudsburg: Association for Computational Linguistics; 2015. pp. 117–126. DOI: 10.18653/v1/S15-1013.

[22] Luan Y, Ostendorf M, Hajishirzi H Scientific information extraction with semi-supervised neural tagging. In: Palmer M, Hwa R, Riedel S, editors. Proceedings of the 2017 Conference on Empirical Methods in Natural Language Processing (EMNLP); 2017 Sep; Copenhagen, Denmark. Stroudsburg: Association for Computational Linguistics; 2017. pp. 2641–2651. DOI: 10.18653/v1/D17-1279.

[23] Lin JCW, Shao Y, Djenouri Y, Yun U. ASRNN: A recurrent neural

network with an attention model for sequence labeling. Knowledge-Based Systems. 2021; **212**. 106548. DOI: 10.1016/j.knosys.2020.106548.

[24] Meng R, Yuan X, Wang T, Brusilovsky P, Trischler A, He D Does order matter? An empirical study on generating multiple keyphrases as a sequence. arXiv preprint arXiv:1909.03590. 2022

[25] Lewis M, Liu Y, Goyal N, Ghazvininejad M, Mohamed A, Levy O, Stoyanov V, Zettlemoyer L BART: Denoising sequence-to-sequence pre-training for natural language generation, translation, and comprehension. arXiv preprint arXiv:1910.13461. 2019.

[26] Issa B, Jasser MB, Chua HN, Hamzah M A comparative study on embedding models for keyword extraction using KeyBERT method. In: 2023 IEEE 13th International Conference on System Engineering and Technology (ICSET); 2023 Oct; Kuala Lumpur, Malaysia. IEEE; 2023. pp. 40–45.

[27] Babayigit B, Sattuf H. BERT-based keyword extraction model for the Turkish language. Neural Computing & Applications. 2025;**37**(16):9807–9819. DOI: 10.1007/s00521-025-11103-x.

[28] Ayan E, Arslan R, Zengin MS, Duru H, Salman S, Bardak B Turkish keyphrase extraction from web pages with BERT. In: Proceedings of the 2021 IEEE 29th Signal Processing and Communications Applications Conference (SIU); 2021 Jun. IEEE; 2021. pp. 1–4. DOI: 10.1109/SIU53274.2021.9477842

[29] Arzu M, Aydoğan M. Comparison of transformer-based Turkish models for question-answering task. Balkan Journal of Electrical and Computer Engineering. 2025;**12**(4):387–393. DOI: 10.17694/bajece.1576976.

[30] Aydın Ö, Kantarcı H. Türkçe anahtar sözcük çıkarımında LSTM ve BERT tabanlı modellerin karşılaştırılması. Bilgisayar Bilimleri Ve Mühendisligi Dergisi. 2024;**17**(1):9–18. DOI: 10.54525/bbmd.1454220.

[31] Ay B, Ertam F, Fidan G, Aydin G. Turkish abstractive text document summarization using text-to-text transfer transformer. Alexandria Engineering Journal. 2023;**68**:1–13. DOI: 10.1016/j.aej.2023.01.008.

[32] Al-Thubaity A. A novel dataset for Arabic domain specific term extraction and comparative evaluation of BERT-based models for Arabic term extraction. ACM Transactions on Asian and Low-Resource Language Information Processing. 2025;**24**(9): 1–12. DOI: 10.1145/3748323.

[33] Alharbi R, Al-Muhtasab H Arabic keyphrase extraction: Enhancing deep learning models with pre-trained contextual embedding and external features. In: Bouamor H, Al-Khalifa H, Darwish K, Rambow O, Bougares F, Abdelali A, Tomeh N, Khalifa S, Zaghouani W, editors. Proceedings of the Seventh Arabic Natural Language Processing Workshop (WANLP); 2022 Dec; Abu Dhabi, United Arab Emirates (Hybrid). Stroudsburg: Association for Computational Linguistics; 2022. pp. 320–330. DOI: 10.18653/v1/2022.wanlp-1.30.

[34] Al-Qurishi M, Alqaseemi S, Souissi R AraLegal-BERT: A pretrained language model for Arabic legal text. In: Aletras N, Chalkidis I, Barrett L, Goanța C, Preoțiuc-Pietro D, editors.

Proceedings of the Natural Legal Language Processing Workshop 2022; 2022 Dec; Abu Dhabi, United Arab Emirates (Hybrid). Stroudsburg: Association for Computational Linguistics; 2022. pp. 338–344. DOI: 10. 18653/v1/2022.nllp-1.31.

[35] Tami M, Ashqar HI, Elhenawy M Automated question generation for science tests in Arabic language using NLP techniques. arXiv preprint arXiv:2406.08520. 2024.

[36] Bsir B, Zrigui M Deep learning based transformers for keyword extraction. 2024.